NAL MUSEUM GROUP.
Thompson.

For Bob, with whom I have followed
the ETS trail for a long time

Ernest Thompson Seton

THE LIFE AND LEGACY OF AN ARTIST AND CONSERVATIONIST

David L. Witt

Foreword by David Attenborough

GIBBS SMITH

TO ENRICH AND INSPIRE HUMANKIND

First Edition
14 13 12 11 10   5 4 3 2 1

A catalog and exhibition by the Academy for the Love of Learning in
conjunction with the New Mexico History Museum: Santa Fe, May
2010 through May 2011.

Published by
Gibbs Smith
P.O. Box 667
Layton, Utah 84041

1.800.835.4993 orders
www.gibbs-smith.com

Designed and produced by Rudy Ramos
Printed and bound in China
Gibbs Smith books are printed on either recycled, 100% post-
consumer waste, FSC-certified papers or on paper produced from a
100% certified sustainable forest/controlled wood source.

Library of Congress Cataloging-in-Publication Data

Witt, David L., 1951-
  Ernest Thompson Seton : the life and legacy of an artist and
conservationist / David L. Witt ; foreword by David Attenborough.
  — 1st ed.
      p. cm.
  " While this book stands on its own, it also serves as the exhibition
catalog for a nearly yearlong show at the New Mexico History
Museum in Santa Fe"—Pref.
  Includes bibliographical references and index.
  ISBN-13: 978-1-4236-0391-7
  ISBN-10: 1-4236-0391-5
  1. Seton, Ernest Thompson, 1860-1946. 2. Naturalists—United
States—Biography. 3. Naturalists—Canada—Biography.
4. Artists—United States—Biography. 5. Artists—Canada—
Biography. 6. Seton, Ernest Thompson, 1860-1946—Exhibitions.
7. Animals in art—Exhibitions. I. Seton, Ernest Thompson,
1860-1946. II. New Mexico History Museum. III. Title.
  QH31.S48W58 2010
  333.72092—dc22
  [B]
                        2009032976

Contents

Foreword

I was given a copy of *Wild Animals I Have Known* when I was eight. I still have it. It was the most precious book of my childhood. I knew very well that the man who wrote it understood the animals he was writing about with an intimacy, perception, and sympathy that was not equaled by any other author that I had read. And I had already read a lot. It made a great difference to me that he was not only a naturalist and a writer of great power, but also an artist. That could not be said of any of the other authors whose books were on my shelf. These were the portraits of the actual animals described in the text—Raggylug, Lobo, and Wully. They were not pictures dreamed up by someone who had never met them. The footprints that ran up the margins—*especially* the footprints—were almost the real thing, drawn by an expert tracker who knew his way around the prairies. I yearned to go with him so that I could learn something of what he knew.

To my surprise, none of my friends in the school I attended in the English Midlands had ever heard of Ernest Thompson Seton. The copy of the book I had been given was printed in the United States, but it was distributed in Great Britain by a British publisher, so it must have been available at British bookshops. Nonetheless, it seemed that Ernest Thompson Seton was a particular discovery of my own. It was all the more precious for that.

In my country he still remains little known. That is a great pity. He was, as readers of this book will know, much more than a naturalist, an artist, and an author. He became a national figure who had a huge effect on the way people thought about the natural world in North America. He has influenced many people who do not even know his name. He certainly greatly influenced me. It is an honour to introduce this book.

—DAVID ATTENBOROUGH
Richmond, Surrey, UK

Introduction

In 1894, Ernest Thompson Seton invented the realistic animal story—a portrayal of wildlife based on scientific natural history of the animal as it really lived and behaved in the wild. Before this time, animal characters were just humans in animal guise, or served as allegorical figures, or simply behaved in impossible ways. Seton, even when he romanticized the story line, nearly always made his animal heroes behave in a way appropriate for their species—behavior that he had often observed firsthand. This mattered, for in both his fiction and nonfiction, Seton, more than anyone else of his time, demonstrated that wildlife deserve our respect, care, and compassion. More than two million copies of his books have been sold, a substantial record for any writer of natural history. During the first two decades of the twentieth century, he was one of America's most popular lecturers and celebrities, continually traveling to venues in the United States, Canada, and England.

In 1902, Seton founded an outdoor youth education program known as the Woodcraft Indians and later incorporated it as the Woodcraft League. Woodcraft ideas revolutionized and greatly expanded and popularized summer recreational youth camps. Seton's work in outdoor youth education helped spur Robert S. S. Baden-Powell to create the Boy Scouts in England. Seton took a leading role in the formation of the Boy Scouts of America, serving as its Chief Scout for four years. Both men contributed ideas essential to international Scouting. Seton's Woodcraft League took a different track from Scouting, adopting a special focus on American Indian wisdom and craft traditions and a rejection of the military aspects favored by Scouts. Early in the 1900s, Seton became one of the first white defenders of Native rights, a proponent of Indian culture, and a leader in the reappraisal of the contribution of traditional tribal values to American society.

Seton may be best remembered, however, for his contributions to our understanding of nature. His pleas for the preservation of wildlife—in the form of books, articles, and lectures—reached more people than any scientific journal, conservation organization, or individual of the first three decades of the twentieth century. His contributions to natural history included pioneering work in what would become the sciences of ecology and ethology (animal behavior). While he called himself a naturalist, he was, in effect, one of the first field biologists, and the first to publish species range maps. As an illustrator,

Seton invented the far-sight method of bird identification later used in field guides by Roger Tory Peterson and others. His thousands of drawings captured much about the meaning of the lives of animals. As godfather to today's environmental movement, he is as important to wildlife conservation as John Muir is to wilderness preservation.

While this book stands on its own, it also serves as the exhibition catalog for a nearly yearlong show at the New Mexico History Museum in Santa Fe. This venue is appropriate given the importance New Mexico played in Seton's life, from his wolf-hunting days in the 1890s to the establishment of Seton Village in the 1930s. Overlooking the village are the remains of Seton Castle, Seton's home during the last years of his life. In 1965, his widow, Julia, transferred most of his art and natural history collections to the Boy Scouts of America for its newly planned museum at Philmont Scout Ranch, in the mountains west of the Currumpaw Valley. In 2003, the Academy for the Love of Learning, an organization devoted to changing our notions about education, acquired the Castle and its remaining collections from his adopted daughter, Dee Seton Barber. The Academy has built its education center on the opposite side of the castle, including a Seton gallery and research center. The Seton legacy lives strongly.

DLW
Taos, New Mexico

CHAPTER ONE

New Mexico, Part One

In mid-October 1893, a tall, hatless, heavily armed stranger rode by train into the remote, rough, dusty, Old West town of Clayton, New Mexico. With its one hotel, one tree, a surprisingly large population of house cats, and rough Anglo and Mexican cowboys (all of whom carried firearms), entrepreneurs, and dreamers, Clayton could have been the setting for a Sergio Leone spaghetti Western. Although over three hundred miles north of Mexico, Clayton was nonetheless a border town between Latino and Anglo civilizations, a crossing between the end of wilderness and settled lands, a moment in time between the endless frontier and the final end of that frontier. The young wild-haired bounty killer was just another of a type who frequented places such as Clayton. His arrival was an unremarkable event for a town in which the progression from day to day seemed prosaic and routine, where drifters passed through with regularity. Like others of his kind, he came on a mission, accepting money in return for doing some violent, unpleasant, but necessary work for which he claimed a reputation equal to the task. At thirty-three, he almost certainly had more blood on his hands than anyone else in Clayton. None of it was human.

He had been sent by an absentee ranch owner to kill wolves and coyotes. If the locals had asked him where he came from—which, in this kind of town, they probably didn't—Ernest Thompson Seton, then still known as Ernest Evan Thompson, might have told them he was a Canadian who divided his time between his residence in Toronto, exploration of Manitoba, visits to London and Paris (art school), and commercial art work in New York that gave him eye strain, from which he needed rest.

Seton was not the first man who went West to reinvent himself. He was a sensitive painter, but he was also a killer of animals—hundreds of birds and mammals had died by his hand in the name of science. He was also an illustrator, a writer, a scholar, a student of Indian lore, a wilderness explorer and tracker, an ascetic but also a confused and soon to be ex-Christian, and, most importantly, a naturalist.

Above: Clayton, New Mexico, as Seton might have seen it in the 1890s. Photo Archives/ Palace of the Governors.

Left: A formal portrait of Ernest Thompson Seton, 1890. Library and Archives Canada.

A Royal Captive, ink wash
and pen and ink, ca. 1920s.
Philmont Museum.

Seton was an expert wolf killer through his experience with the timber wolves of Canada. The New Mexico cowboys, skeptical of the very concept of a Canadian wolf trapper, at first had their suspicions confirmed by his inability to catch much besides dogs and coyotes. They took note, however, when he dressed in stinking clothes and blood-covered gloves. This method of wolf trapping (reducing the human smell associated with traps and baits) was unknown to them. As always, Seton would spare no effort to be as good as his word, no matter what it cost him. Whether moved by professional ambition in the city or by a need to explore, riding off alone into wild, dangerous country he had never seen before, he came at life with a fearlessness matched by few except the wolves he hunted.

By early 1894, the wolf killer had accomplished several remarkable things in New Mexico. Riding the range, often alone, he rejected his earlier concept of God, he conceptualized the importance of connecting youth to nature, he came upon an idea for a new literary genre, and he began rethinking his habit of killing animals. He met a particular wolf he would name "Lobo," an animal who would bring him fame and make possible much of his future success. Lobo and the wolf pack of which he was a part awoke in Seton a conscience, a personal transformation he would share with the world.

Lobo, whom Seton named some weeks after their meeting, was one of several cattle-eating wolves plaguing the local Anglo and Mexican ranchers. Seton, who would later become the founder of the wildlife conservation movement, took a negative view of wolves at the time. He used trickery and treachery against an animal whose weaknesses were loyalty and fidelity. Lobo, however, proved more powerful than Seton could have guessed, inadvertently contributing to two of the great American social movements of the twentieth century.

After just under four months' time, Seton suddenly left New Mexico. Back at his home in Toronto, he immediately began writing the story of his wolf hunt. He had already penned a few articles on birds and other subjects, but after reviewing his personal journal, he found in Lobo his first serious subject. He understood the epic nature of a story about man against beast. Lobo's was a compelling tale where the wolf was the hero and the people—even the author himself—were the villains. "The King of Currumpaw, A Wolf Story" appeared in the November 1894 edition of *Scribner's Magazine*, just months after Seton's return from New Mexico. Four years later it was included in *Wild Animals I Have Known* as "Lobo, the King of Currumpaw."

Reflecting upon his violent actions in New Mexico, Seton began his transition from wildlife killer to wildlife protector, a hunter who would come to loathe trapping and high-powered rifles. He was a scientist who psychologically and spiritually moved from a Cartesian objectification of animals as senseless specimens to a view of animals as individuals with motivations, feelings, and personalities much like our own. It might not have been reasonably predicted that Seton's encounter with a half dozen canine predators would change the world. But through them, he came to understand that wild nature and its creatures are essential to establishing our own identity and a moral basis for how we live. Seton showed that we are not fundamentally different from wolves and other animals. We are different only by degree, making us not *apart* from nature, but rather a part of it. The concept is as radical today as it was in Seton's time.

"These stories are true. Although I have left the strict line of historical truth in many places, the animals in this book were all real characters. They lived the lives I have depicted, and showed the stamp of heroism and personality more strongly by far than it has been in the power of my pen to tell."
—*Wild Animals I Have Known*

The Currumpaw

The Currumpaw (or Corrumpa) Creek east of Clayton is one of many look-alike watersheds whose infrequent floods flow eastward away from higher country, including, most notably, the rocky height of Capulin Volcano National Monument, a perfect volcanic cone. While it is today bisected more or less west to east by US 64, this is country where arroyos cut deep canyons and form beautiful and unexpected features, like the high waterfall just outside Folsom, not far from Capulin. Except for the occasional dark green forest atop one of the old volcanoes, the hills of this semi-arid grassland appear gray-brown most of the year. One might think that most of the life died out in this remote ranch country about the time the volcanoes went extinct long ago. And yet, upon a closer look, there is contradictory evidence. In the spring, small, bright yellow sunflowers appear amid the sheltering rocks. Grasses—dull colored in dry times, rich green in wet periods—support an abundance of wildlife. In early autumn, hundreds of millions of ladybugs crawl over the windy summit of Capulin. In the quiet hours of most nights, the yipping of coyotes echoes through the cañons.

There is more about this place than meets the eye. The trained naturalist, a person who studies the relationship of life forms to their environment, can reveal its secrets. Seton wrote about the area in three early New Mexico stories—"Lobo," "The Pacing Mustang," and "The Kangaroo Rat"—showing his remarkable ability as an observer and passionate advocate of wild nature:

Left and Facing: Union
County, New Mexico,
1975. David L. Witt.

The place seemed uninviting to a stranger from the lush and fertile prairies of Manitoba, but the more I saw of it the more it was revealed a paradise. For every cottonwood of the straggling belt that the river used to mark its doubtful course across the plain, and every dwarfed and spiny bush and weedy copse, was teeming with life. And every day and every night I made new friends, or learned new facts about the mudland denizens.

Below: *Bird's Eye View of the Mound.* Burrow illustration for "The Kangaroo Rat" in *Lives of the Hunted,* pen and ink, 1893. Philmont Museum.

During his first weeks in northeastern New Mexico, Seton lived in a ramshackle stone cabin along the Leon Creek in what is now Union County. Suspecting that this dry country might support more mammal activity at night than during the day, Seton "swept clean" two pathways around the dwelling to learn by tracks what transpired during the dark hours. He learned of an encounter between a bobcat and a skunk, the meeting coming to the chagrin of the former: "There was evidence, too, that the Bobcat quickly said (in Bobcat, of course), 'I beg pardon, I mistook you for a rabbit, but will

never again make such a mistake.'" (Seton defied convention by always capitalizing the names of the animals he wrote about.) Lobo, Seton said, left his tracks outside the cabin at night while the human occupants slept. Jackrabbits, cottontails, and coyotes ran about as well, but particularly intriguing was the multitude of little circular tracks, no more than indentations in the sand, which often accumulated in huge numbers. Perplexed, he thought back to his Celtic roots and the Old Country, where such a phenomenon might have been attributed to the denizens of faerie. Here that wouldn't work, but it did set up for Seton the conflict of "Arcadie" versus "Scientia," the fanciful (or imaginary) against the empirical. Regarding the fanciful world of belief, Seton wrote, "But for me, alas! it was impossible, for long ago, when my soul came to the fork in the trail marked on the left 'To Arcadie,' and on the right 'To Scientia,' I took the flinty, upland right-hand path. I had given up my fayland eyes for—for I do not know what."

As is better known today than in Seton's time, kangaroo rats have the exceptional ability to bounce about the desert, using their long tails for balance. Found throughout much of New Mexico, they spend daylight hours underground, with burrow entrances beneath spiny cacti or yucca, which effectively deter digging coyotes. Seton caught a specimen, telling it, "I . . . am ready to sit at those microscopic and beautiful feet of yours and learn." The best way to understand the home life of a burrowing animal is to dig up its home and make a diagram of the tunnel and nest arrangements. (Seton may have been the first naturalist to publish burrow diagrams.) An indefatigable, even obsessive, worker, Seton could spend hours digging up a rat nest. Although he did not say so, shoveling sand may have been a needed diversion from his increasingly fruitless hunt for wolves. A rat was easy to trap and fascinating to keep as a pet, at least until it figured out how to mound dirt to the top of its wooden cage and gnaw its way to freedom. Seton was not just impressed but delighted at the ingenuity of the little sprite. He seems not to have previously understood the wonderful individuality that even a rat might exhibit.

Unlike most of his work, "The Kangaroo Rat" was not a short story, but instead a straightforward account of his observations. It wasn't just a work of science, but rather an homage to the rodent. As much as Seton tried to remain objective, his attributions of emotions such as "joy" to a rat put him somewhat outside the realm of normal science.

At the same time, Seton chronicled the manic search for a black stallion in "The Pacing Mustang," foreshadowing one of his finest stories, "Krag, the Kootenay Ram," three years later. Both the Mustang and Lobo stories established one of the great literary themes of Seton's career: the relentless and more or less demented persecution

of animals by humankind. These stories make clear the notion that the animal is a sentient individual, a being possessed with awareness, concerns, desires, and feelings. In "The Pacing Mustang," the Pacer is hunted down simply because of its dedication to freedom, and the irrational fear the cowboys seem to have of its untamed state. The horse is morally superior to those who would capture it. In this Seton foresaw, decades before the emergence of an environmental movement, the dire consequences for a civilization determined to wipe out its natural surroundings.

From this the first corral and ranch-house were in sight. The man rejoiced, but the Mustang gathered his remaining strength for one more desperate dash. Up, up the grassy slope from the trail he went, defied the swinging, slashing rope and the gunshot fired in air, a vain attempt to turn his frenzied course. Up, up and on, above the sheerest cliff he dashed then sprang away into the vacant air, down—down—two hundred feet to fall, and land upon the rocks below, a lifeless wreck—but free.

Seton did not have the good fortune of an advanced formal education, but no one possessed a greater thirst for knowledge about nature than he. Years of tramping the wilds of the far north had made of him a superb outdoorsman and an observer of

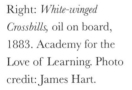

Right: *White-winged Crossbills*, oil on board, 1883. Academy for the Love of Learning. Photo credit: James Hart.

Facing: *Away Went the Mustang at His Famous Pace.* Illustration for "The Pacing Mustang" in *Wild Animals I Have Known.* Philmont Museum.

Above: *Landscape with Whitetail Deer*, oil on canvas, 1893. Academy for the Love of Learning. Photo credit: James Hart.

Facing: Kansas coyote hunt, stereo photo, n.d. Library of Congress.

wildlife almost without peer. Besides being an excellent marksman, he was a tireless hiker, an experienced horseman, and a gifted student of Native American woodsmen. But he could never have been content to remain a simple backwoodsman; his supreme intellect, outgoing personality, and towering ambition would force him to become a success in two worlds—the wilderness and the arts and literary society of New York. Of the two, he preferred the former, but the seduction of celebrity—his own, as well as the association with other famous people—drove him mercilessly.

The cowboys in New Mexico did not know that Seton already had a burgeoning reputation among the leading naturalists and scientists of the United States and Canada. In the 1880s he began collecting bird specimens for the Smithsonian and made the acquaintance of the leading wildlife scientists of the time. In 1885 he wrote a *Key to the Orders of the Canadian Birds*, with short text and simple line drawings to make sense of the feathered multitude. His massive amount of observation time led to his publishing in 1897 "flying descriptions" by which birders could identify birds in flight at a distance, a useful skill particularly with hawks and waterfowl, and one that would become a staple of many bird-identification guides. Not only was this a first in the literature, but

Seton also pointed out that birds (as well as jackrabbits and other mammals) are often "protectively" colored when at rest to stay hidden and "directively" marked when in motion, providing a warning signal or a follow-me message to others of their own kind. These same observational skills also made Seton a good trapper. Just before his New Mexico assignment, he wrote promotional copy for a wolf-trap sales brochure, "How To Catch Wolves": "Giving the latest and most successful methods as practiced by the professional trappers of the North American continent."

Wolves had been hunted in New Mexico for a long time, with a fair level of success. The animals that remained had learned through horrible lessons the ways of survival in the world of man. They hid during the day when men with rifles were about and instead hunted at night; Seton would go on in later years to chronicle behavioral changes in several mammals occurring as a direct result of encounters with rifle-armed men. Wolves learned the smell of strychnine, arsenic, cyanide, and steel traps, and generally avoided these instruments of death. Seton nonetheless promised to eliminate the wolves, but killing has its price, and it is the shallow man who can look into the eyes of a morally superior enemy and not come away changed in some fundamental way, even if victorious over that enemy. He did not underestimate wolf intelligence. In the wolf-trap promotional brochure, he wrote:

> *The Common Wolf (*Canis lupus*) is a native to the whole Northern Hemisphere . . .*
> *it is everywhere of the same character, and is everywhere hated and feared as a devastator*
> *of the flocks and herds . . . The wolf hunter has to cope with an animal of almost human*
> *intelligence, an animal without superior in sagacity among all the wild beasts of the chase,*
> *and one which will tax his utmost ability to circumvent.*

Seton then went on to explain how to kill wolves. By following his instructions, "It will usually then be quite easy to follow his track and kill your wolf." But nothing about hunting the Currumpaw wolves would prove "quite easy."

The wolf did not take on its role vis-à-vis humankind by choice. Seton figured this out during his New Mexico trip. The gray wolf (*Canis lupus*) had got along for thousands of years eating antelope, elk, deer, and even bison. Of the New Mexico wolves, few were known to have attained size much greater than a German shepherd, usually under eighty pounds. (Seton found an unsubstantiated claim of one wolf weighing one hundred and fifty pounds, a weight he assigned to Lobo, who was actually much smaller.) But as the area became more populated by man (and as sport hunters killed off much of their natural prey), wolves faced a simple choice: kill cows or starve to death. The destruction of cattle meant financial loss to the cattle business, already economically marginal in the arid Southwest. Every cow lost to wolf predation meant scarce dollars gone. When Seton arrived in New Mexico, he sided with the ranchers; after he left, he sided with the wolves.

The Cowboys

In his autobiography, *Trail of an Artist-Naturalist,* Seton dwells for a moment in the New Mexico of 1893, telling several tales about the fascinating characters he met there. One of these stories was about the Yankee from Massachusetts, "Chawles Fitzwohltah was his name, as he pronounced it." Seton termed him "The Dude," and wrote that he was the object of some fun to the rollicking and sometimes dangerous cowboys and gunmen who frequented the last days of the Western frontier. The Dude, having suddenly decided to become a lawman—based on novels he had read and the Buffalo Bill–type costume he purchased in Chicago on his first trip West—is entirely underestimated by the bad men he encounters. They get the short end of every fight they get into with the soft-spoken easterner.

In reality, there was no such man. There were two.

Claiming a fear of libel suits, Seton combined two characters from his New Mexico days to come up with The Dude. One of these men, Charlie Sandford, was a big fellow who wore showman cowboy clothes. Nothing more about him has turned up. The other, Stuart Hayt Patterson, really *was* an accidental lawman. In his later life he wrote, but didn't publish, an autobiography that included a brief section about Seton. He and Seton had in common a desire to reinvent themselves, and if anywhere in America was an appropriate place for that task, it was the Southwest. Remote places often lend themselves to such transitions—think of the archeologists Gertrude Bell and T. E. Lawrence, who became literal kingmakers in Iraq and Jordan.

Patterson, a native of New York, had followed a girlfriend to Seattle, sailed to San Francisco to find work, and, when neither career nor romance worked out, drifted on to the Brazos River country in Texas. He spent two months cowboying, but few jobs are at once so tiring, dangerous, and low paying as ranch hand. He did not hesitate when offered the job of Chief Deputy United States Marshal. He sported a Wyatt Earp–type mustache, and despite his youth and Eastern accent, he looked the part of a Western lawman, thus serving as a good model for Seton's cowboy stories. Patterson would go on to a successful business career, leveraging his roughhouse days in Texas and New Mexico into the toughness needed by the early twentieth-century capitalist.

In the spring of 1893, while still in Texas, Patterson met Lewis V. Fitz Randolph, a "prominent citizen" from Plainfield, New Jersey. Patterson himself had once lived in Plainfield. Fitz Randolph happened to own a ranch in northeastern New Mexico, to which he invited Patterson for a visit. They rode from Dallas to Clayton via the Fort Worth and Denver Railroad, then by horse to the L Cross F Ranch on Penabetos Creek. Mount Dora and Sierra Grande, extinct volcanoes, loomed to the north over the Currumpaw Valley. Fitz Randolph wanted an assistant ranch manager to keep an eye on his minority share co-owner, H. M. Foster. Patterson got himself a new job.

Around the same time, Seton, who divided his time between Toronto and New York, was also making the acquaintance of Fitz Randolph. He had earlier met one of the five Fitz Randolph daughters, Virginia, in Paris, where he had been an art student. During the summer of 1893, he found frequent excuses to head out to the Fitz Randolph house, where he enjoyed the company of another daughter, Caroline, "an outstanding beauty." By early fall he was managing to spend time independently with both Virginia and Caroline. In mid-September, he noted in his journal Caroline's petulance over a dispute with one of her professors at Wellesley College. He wryly added, "She continued all day. Another idol shattered."

A photograph of Stuart H. Patterson as a cowboy, New Mexico, 1893, reproduced in the *Guaranty News*. Academy for the Love of Learning.

Romance was not in the cards, but a trip to New Mexico soon was. Tired of New York and the demands of a career as an illustrator, Seton learned about the ranch and the problem of wolf predation during one of his talks with Fitz Randolph. In his autobiography, he noted, "Oh, how I did long to go on a campaign against those wolves! I knew I could meet them and beat them, but I dared not take the time. My duties held me bound. I was working all day at the easel, and every night till late at my desk." Plagued by headaches from stress and overwork, he was advised by a doctor to take a break or risk losing his sight. Fitz Randolph told him, "If you will go to my ranch in New Mexico, and show the boys some way of combating the big cattle-killing wolves, I will pay your expenses, and let you make whatever you can out of bounties and hides. But you must promise to spend at least a month on the ground at the work." Seton responded by letter.

October 6th, 1893.
Lewis V. Fitz Randolph, Esq.

Dear Sir:

I have decided to accept the offer you kindly made me at our last meeting—and will be ready to start for your ranch on a two months wolf hunt in about a week—To repeat—I am to go out to your place in New Mexico for two months—and during that time am to do what I can to kill off the wolves myself—as well as influence the ranchmen of the neighborhood to begin some sort of organized war on these pests.

I am to have the skins of what I kill and also the bounties.

You are to pay for my ammunition and poison and meet any railroad expenses between here and New Mexico and return, also provide me with a horse while there, and with my keep on the ranch.

As I think it will be advisable to take a larger quantity of poison than I can use myself—so as to be able to provide other ranches—I may have to make a considerable outlay here—perhaps ten or fifteen dollars. I shall not take much ammunition as it is not much account among wolves. The railway ticket from here is a trifle over fifty dollars so that it would take seventy-five or eighty dollars to thoroughly equip me and land me there.

I suppose I should be right in taking just such clothing as I wear here in the winter.

Is there any difficulty in collecting wolf bounties? Are they paid out in Clayton?

I suppose that as long as I am doing a fair amount of destruction I shall not be bound to spend all my time wolf hunting as I should like to do a little sketching.

This letter sounds a trifle judicial, but I suppose it is well for me to know beforehand just exactly what is expected of me.

Again thanking you for your kindness in making this offer and giving me the opportunity for a really needed outing, I am sir

Yours very sincerely,
Ernest E. Thompson

Working at the Fitz Randolph ranch, Patterson received a letter dated October 10 from his boss discussing various business matters. It read, "I have just received a letter from my wolf-killing friend, Mr. Ernest E. Thompson, of which I enclose a copy. I have written him to start for New Mexico at once. He is a man of intelligence and refinement, but accustomed to rough it." Enclosed in Fitz Randolph's letter to Patterson was Seton's original letter. Although new to the territory, Patterson had been told that wolves (coyotes and gray wolves) killed half the "calf crop" each year, the difference between making a profit and taking a loss on the ranching operation. "The coyotes," he wrote, were no problem except that "when the lobos made a kill and had eaten what they wanted, the coyotes finished what was left, with the result that every time a lobo wolf was hungry he made a fresh kill."

Neither Patterson nor Foster was impressed by Seton's impending arrival. They didn't bother to go all the way to Clayton to meet him. Instead, Patterson arranged for Seton to get a ride with a mail carrier to the ranch of a cowboy, Jack Brooks (identified as "Jim Bender" in Seton's autobiography), who lived along Leon Creek in the shack from which Seton would later observe the kangaroo rats.

Brooks was paid four dollars a week for feeding and housing the Canadian wolf killer. He was to have served as Seton's cook, but it didn't work out. Seton recalled, "Bender [that is, Brooks] hated to get up early. My habit was to rise about seven; he would lie abed until nine, unless dragged out. The difference it made to me was the preparing of breakfast." Seton ended up fixing breakfast for them both—day after day. Tiring of this, Seton "made a nice batch of biscuit for myself, then a special batch for Jim. But I made his with washing soda instead of baking soda." He followed up by putting salt in Bender's coffee the next morning, and then axle grease on Bender's steak. The cowboy responded with "unparliamentary" language, then grudgingly agreed to resume his paid responsibilities as cook. People have been murdered for less provocation, so it was probably just as well that Patterson finally decided to check up on the wolf hunter:

Above: A tintype group shot, with Seton at back left. Library and Archives Canada.

Facing: *Tempting the Coyote.* Illustration for "The Kangaroo Rat" in *Lives of the Hunted,* gouache, 1899. Philmont Museum.

A couple of weeks later I happened to be down that way and thought I would look him up . . . When I met him he was lonesome and half starved living with Bender. I suggested that if he wanted to share my bed in the dining-room he could come to the ranch and operate from there, an offer which he accepted with alacrity.

Besides looking after Seton's well being, Patterson later penned the only significant account of Seton's time in New Mexico, describing the young naturalist's appearance and demeanor.

Seton had a great mass of hair and never wore a hat—he was the first man I ever saw always go bareheaded. He was a quiet, modest man, respected by the cowboys. At first they thought him too finicky in his methods because of the great care and precautions before setting traps or putting out baits. For this purpose he had an old suit of clothes, shoes and gloves, all thoroughly saturated with cattle blood, an outfit always kept outside the house and never worn except during these operations. This reduced the human smell on traps and bait to a minimum and, so far as possible, substituted the scent of animal blood.

He was as precise in all his dealings, as his letter to Mr. Randolph shows. Later he told me that during his trip from Toronto he restricted himself to one meal a day, costing twenty-five cents, except in a single yielding to extravagance when he indulged in two meals in one day at the cost of half a dollar. There was no need for such drastic economy, but he was practising [sic] his customary thrift, learned by necessity in his early struggles.

As there wasn't much doing at the ranch during this period, I frequently rode with him to examine his traps. He had no trouble exterminating the coyotes, but for a considerable time he was unable to get any lobo wolves, even with all the care and experience.

Regrettably, Patterson left New Mexico on a trip east in January 1894 and was not on hand to witness Seton's encounter with Lobo. But during their short time working together, Patterson came to respect Seton enough to lend him a camera and Marlin .44 rifle—the ones Seton used later that month. Patterson knew that Seton would return both.

When Seton became an old man, he began recording stories about some of the cowboy characters he met in New Mexico. Writing in the late 1930s, he appears to have called up the events of the 1890s purely from memory. Many of these stories read like tall tales; from today's standpoint, it is difficult to know just how much truth they convey. In some of these, he is a player, such as during an encounter with the alluring "Belle Boulton," who nearly gets him killed by a man whom she wants to make jealous.

Ernest Seton-Thompson

Or his run-in with the cattle rustler "Big Tannerey," who tricked Seton into showing him how to make a counterbrand from a legitimate brand—that is, altering one brand into another. When Tannerey bragged about his teacher, Seton later claimed that he had to leave New Mexico to escape arrest.

Amid the frivolous accounts are two serious ones that, to whatever extent they are true, are important. A cowboy from a nearby ranch, feeling unwell, mistook a bottle of poison, possibly strychnine, for the quinine he had intended to take. Three agonizing minutes later, the man's suffering ended with his death. This is an event of great significance, yet it is not mentioned in Seton's journal. Seton had written to Fitz Randolph his intention to distribute poison to the other ranches. Did the cowboy die from poison provided by Seton? Also not mentioned in Seton's journal, but attested to by Patterson, was the accidental poisoning of dozens of dogs by carcasses baited by Seton for coyotes and wolves. Given the relatively fast action of the strychnine, poisoned animals were nearly always found as carcasses. Seton unemotionally noted in his journal that a shore lark died on November 19 from one of his poison traps. His attitude began to change when he witnessed the horrible process of a coyote dying from his bait. He rode toward the violently convulsing animal, intending to shoot it. His usual skill with the rifle failed, and the animal began to run and vomit until finally disgorging enough of the poison to perhaps recover and disappear out into the brush. He recorded, "I had often found my poison victims with gashes on loins and on limbs; I knew now that these were self-inflicted in their agony." This marks what might be thought of as the first step in Seton's conversion. "What right," he asked, "has man to inflict such horrible agony on fellow beings, merely because they do a little damage to his material interests? It is not right; it is horrible—horrible—hellish! And I put out no more poison baits."

Seton was familiar with a medieval story about the conversion of the seventh-century priest Hubertus. In the story, the priest pursues a stag in spirited hunt, passionate to make a kill. As he is about to dispatch the magnificent creature, a voice warns him, "Hubert, unless thou turnest to the Lord, and leadest an Holy life, thou shalt quickly go down into hell." To his further astonishment, Hubert sees a crucifix suspended between the creature's antlers. These signs are impossible to ignore, so he calls off the hunt and transfers his true passions to the benefit of Christ. Subsequently, both hunters and preservationists have considered him a patron saint. Compare this to a passage in Seton's 1899 story, "The Trail of the Sandhill Stag." The protagonist, young Yan (Seton's alter ego), has similarly given his all in the pursuit of a deer he needs to kill.

"Shoot, shoot, shoot now! This is what you have toiled for," said a faint and fading voice, and spoke no more.

But Yan remembered the night when he, himself, run down, had turned to face the hunting wolves, he remembered too that night when the snow was red with crime, and now between him and the other there he dimly saw a vision of an agonizing, dying doe, with great, sad eyes, that only asked, 'What harm have I done you?' A change came over him, and every thought of murder went from Yan as they gazed in each other's eyes—and hearts. Yan could not look him in the eyes and take his life, and different thoughts and a wholly different concept of the Stag, coming—coming—long coming—had come.

The Revival

While Seton was coming to a new view of animals, he was also coming to a new view of religion. He intended to publish this aspect of his conversion in his autobiography, but it was instead included as part of a larger unpublished work that was a rant against the leadership of the Boy Scouts of America. He published only one section of this chapter, what seemed no more than an amusing story about a cowboy at a revival meeting. But the larger point he had originally intended to make was about an important shift in his own attitudes about religion, one also relating to his developing views on education and conservation.

My people were devotees of a strange school of theology, which began by assuming the total depravity of all human nature, by definitely announcing that all human beings were born fore-doomed to hell unless redeemed and saved in some miraculous manner, and that all human instincts were the direct instigation of the devil, therefore must be stamped out. They are the old Adam.

But I early became a rebel. Guided by common sense, by observation, by zoology, and above all, by the sayings of the Greatest of all Teachers, I began with the assumption that All children come here direct from God and are pure as God can make them. We do not have to reform them, but rather to keep them from being deformed.

In other words my home teachers held that all children were bound for hell. I preferred to follow the great Teacher who proclaimed, "That of such is the Kingdom of heaven."

Against these total depravity preachments, I was in continual rebellion, I could not see it. If God made the birds to sing and nest-build on Sunday, why was I a reprobate for watching and enjoying the same? The answer was, "Because I was a reprobate." The conflict became so acute that I left home in my teens, and never returned.

I went out West, and lived the ordinary life of the Plains—hunting, camping, ranching, etc., and ever as I rode, these things were revolved in my mind—for I did not consider them as of small account. The fact that my mother held to them gave them importance.

Soon and often, I met with this puzzle: When some new situation arose, I found that my inborn impulses were better guides than my judgment. How could that be, if my inborn impulses were the promptings of the devil? The answer was the one I heard at home: Because I was a freak, a reprobate. But I found that other men were freaks of this type. And ever the number grew, till I began to believe that we freaks had a majority.

Then occurred an incident that to me turned out important. A revivalist preacher came among us. We had no church in which to receive him, but the school house was available. There the cattlemen and ranchers assembled to hear his gruesome message. We cowboys were a pretty wild lot fifty years ago. All carried guns and used them when they thought necessary. I think there was but one important influence for good among these wild ones; that was love and respect for our mothers. If any of us went to church, the main idea was so we could write home and say "Dear Mother: I went to church last Sunday and heard a sermon that made me think a lot about you."

Imagine the effect when that Preacher began in good set and familiar terms: "All we were shapen in Iniquity, and in Sin did our mothers conceive us."

Up jumped a wild cowboy and yelled: "Damn your soul, my mother didn't conceive me in no such way. My mother was a good woman. I ain't agoin' to set by and let no man slander my mother." Then he flashed his gun on the preacher and yelled: "Get down on you knees now, and take that all back, or I'll blow you full of holes."

The trembling little preacher got down on his knees and "Took it all back," he "Didn't mean a word of it."

"Then what in hell did ye say it for?"

He didn't know, only he had been taught to say it that way.

"Well you better not blow off that stuff around here."

Then the meeting broke up, nobody saved but the preacher. But the thought did not break up. That wild cowboy had given exact expression to a thought that all of us dimly sensed, "What kind of religion is it that puts the stamp of crime on every God appointed natural human relationship?" And the answer that presented itself was, "It isn't religion. It is the most degrading, lowest depth of priestcraft superstition."

Yes, that revival meeting set a lot of us to thinking. What's the meaning of it all? . . . "Were we shapen in iniquity?" "Is every human impulse the direct inspiration of the devil?" These were the questions that would not [be forced] down. All my early training said, "Yes." All my instincts said, "No." The hills swept by, and the steers or wild game galloped on, and still I pondered as I rode. Slowly, very slowly, came the light.

The Hunt

It may be that night is darkest before dawn; this at least would prove true for Seton. The story of his wolf hunt is essential to understanding everything else that happened in his life. He kept a daily journal during his four months in New Mexico that would serve as the basis for the Lobo story and several nonfiction accounts of his time in the state. In one of these accounts, he stated his goals, and added one of his first comments on the vanishing wildlife of the West.

. . . It became my habit to announce a purpose, to some extent arrange a program, before commencing a trip. When, therefore, I set out for New Mexico, in Oct. 1893 seeking for a rest after overlong hours of study, I resolved that my first object should be to kill 15 gray wolves, my second to ascertain accurately the weight of all large animals killed that I should meet with, and thirdly to sketch the tracks of all the quadrupeds of the region.

The first man to ask me the object of my journeying was an old Kansas farmer, whom I met in the train, after conversing about the country in general he said, "What are you coming out to this country for anyhow?"

"Oh, I replied, I wish to knock around and see if I can get any shooting."

To this he said, shaking his head dubiously, "No, no! We be a very peaceable people out here. You won't see no shooting. You must go to New York, or Chicago, or some big city and hang around the barrooms if you want to see any shooting."

When I explained that I meant shooting game he rejoined, "Oh its hunting you mean, well thar ain't much of that, a few ducks and snipes maybe. Everything else has been killed off."

Imagine this in the land that ten years ago was the home of the Elk and the Buffalo, the Grisly [sic] and the Antelope!

Lobo & Blanca 189

Above: *Lobo and Blanca,*
ink wash and pen and ink,
1894. Philmont Museum.

Right: *Buffalo and Wolf,* oil
on board, 1893. Philmont
Museum.

Fitz Randolph had given Seton a check for $80 on September 30 to pay for the trip. Of this, according to his journal accounting, $32.65 went for railroad fares, $6.54 for rifle ammunition, $5 for two and a half days at the Clayton hotel, and fifty cents for dinner there, along with miscellaneous expenses, adding up to just over $72. He had with him a book by W. Hamilton Chase, *Camp Life in the Woods and Tricks of Trapping and Trap Making*, a comprehensive look at how to trap many kinds of animals, from moles to bears, with instructions on camping, cabin construction, and other sorts of Woodcraft lore. Thus prepared with the needed stuff, he began interviewing the locals to find out about wolves: "From conversations with the men I learn that wolves are very destructive yet scarce and so difficult to kill that it is not worth while making a business of it." They talked only of "cattle and politics." Some of them would remember his visit for a long time afterward. One Clayton journalist, A. W. Thompson, wrote Seton forty-five years later to reminisce.

> *You will recall perhaps my meeting you in Clayton, New Mexico, in 1893, and your visits to my store, directly across the street from the Clayton House (run by Harry Wells) . . . I remember one or two evening calls you made me when, after the shades were drawn, I listened to your experiences, your plans to kill wolves, and other no less glamorous relations . . . Does your recollection take you back to a morning when, after a light fall of snow, you escorted me to the edge of town . . . and asked me to follow with you, the track of a rabbit, as the animal ran here and there (during the night), pointing where he stopped, went on, jumped, and finally disappeared?*

While he had come to kill wolves, Seton found time to observe the peculiar hopping of jackrabbits—on every fourth bound they leap upward on their hind legs to get a better view of their surroundings. He shot at prairie dogs but found that even if he did hit one, it would fall out of reach into its hole. The rodents were not much threatened by him, as the cartridges for his new Marlin would fail more often than not. He spotted a tumbleweed from a distance, at first mistaking the movement of the unique plant for that of a fox. He also took time to sketch rough-hewn Clayton and its surroundings; it probably reminded him of similar places from his earlier life in Manitoba. His purpose on this trip, however, was more serious than following bunnies and prairie dogs. He began the Lobo story with a description of the place and his purpose.

> *Currumpaw is a vast cattle range in northern New Mexico. It is a land of rich pastures and teeming flocks and herds, a land of rolling mesas and precious running waters that at length*

unite in the Currumpaw River, from which the whole region is named. And the king whose despotic power was felt over its entire extent was an old gray wolf.

Old Lobo, or the king, as the Mexicans called him, was the gigantic leader of a remarkable pack of gray wolves, which had ravaged the Currumpaw Valley for a number of years. All the shepherds and ranchmen knew him well, and, wherever he appeared with his trusty band, terror reigned supreme among the cattle, and wrath and despair among their owners. Old Lobo was a giant among wolves, and was cunning and strong in proportion to his size.

Seton set to work from his first day on the L Cross F ranch, learning his way around from Brooks and other cowboys, confident in his ability to catch and kill wolves. Then came a surprise—weeks passed with almost no contact with the animals. These predators, he wrote in his story, "scorned all hunters, derided all poisons, and continued for at least five years [before Seton's arrival] to exact their tribute from the Currumpaw ranchers to the extent, many said, of a cow each day." The reason for this was that the wolves, at huge cost to themselves, had learned the necessity of eating only

Right: *Black Wolf of the Currumpaw*, oil on board, 1893. Philmont Museum.

Facing: *Lobo*, oil on board, 1893 and 1946. Philmont Museum.

Lobo
by E.T Seton
1893 – 1946

Blanca, oil on board, 1893 and 1946. Philmont Museum.

fresh-killed meat. Seton "heard of a wolf hunter, Joe Callis, who killed 106 gray wolves here in 6 weeks." Callis was unable to catch the few remaining wolves. Their days were nonetheless numbered. Wolves would hang on in parts of New Mexico into the 1950s before extirpation, but the sad fact was that Seton was already too late. The frontier was coming to a close—the last wild wolves and the last unfenced lands were being killed, rounded up, tamed, whatever was expedient.

Nonetheless, Seton tried his hand at poisoning. Dogs and coyotes, it seems, were slower learners than the remaining wolves. Brooks reported having seen a distant wolf on October 27, but even finding tracks would prove difficult until the second week in November, when Seton made a note in his journal: "Went in afternoon with JB. To trail for wolves. Went first towards Clapham then SE, then NE towards the first Lake & home straight across country." He made sketches of wolf footprints. The tracks were three and a half inches long and eleven inches apart. At least they were now searching in the right area. Seton wrote out a list of Spanish names for animals, including "Wolf—Lobo." A few days later he thought he saw his first wolves, but he marked the notation with a question mark. He set or checked wolf baits every day, even disguising his presence at one of these by using a dead skunk as a drag to cover his scent. Then he wrote in his journal of his first close contact.

> *Nov. 16 Wolf seen at bait site.*
>
> *Nov. 18 Two wolves seen.*
>
> *Nov. 19 Went around my drags—two lobos & [?] coyotes had followed—five coyotes had taken baits—but I got only two of them. The Lobos [?] at the baits—urinated on them & went on. Something had eaten about 20 lbs of the steer but carefully avoided the poisoned parts. One lobo track measured 2 1/2 x 3 1/2 inches. The house dog was also among the victims. There seems to be no difficulty in getting the wolves to follow the drag—but they are extremely fastidious about what they eat.*
>
> *Nov. 24 Went with J.B. to see Joe Callis the Wolf hunter . . . [he] was very obliging in giving me a lot of [?] tips as to killing wolves. He has a [?] lobo alive. It is a ♂ about 8 months old—stands 28 inches height at the apparent shoulder.—no doubt it would lose 4 inches if the hair were pressed down. It is very tame—plays with the dogs . . . about 50 lbs in weight—yet it can drag off a weight of about 60 lbs. Callis says it is almost useless to attempt poisoning old [adult] wolves—there are 3 or 4 on his farm that have been there for years.*

Seton once more sought out Callis—whom he called Joe Calone in the Lobo story—but as of the first of December, he had not come any closer to catching his first wolf. He

"I set out to assemble the fragments that should spell to us the Lives of our Wild Things as they really are—knowing that we had so long been told that they were dumb, brute beasts; suspecting that we ourselves were cowards and liars in so placing them. I have had some shocks and joys in my search for the truth."
—*Lives of Game Animals, Part II*

Wolf perspective study, pencil, n.d. Philmont Museum.

had to admit in the story that "I found that all my efforts had been useless. The old king was too cunning for me." It was at this point that he found some diversion in digging up and drawing the plans for a kangaroo rat burrow; he also collected locoweed, a plant previously unknown to him, and wrote his observations about cowboys, whom he admired except for their excessive drinking when in town. Winter arrived, adding yet another dimension of discomfort to his endless rounds in the nasty task of baiting dead animals with poison. "I was at my wit's end," he recalled in his autobiography, "and I was no nearer to success than any other man." The journal does not give the date when he changed tactics, but he says in his autobiography, "The total failure of the poison left me with one more stratagem, that is, steel traps."

Then, on December 13, the first kill. He gave it the number 653 in his journal.

This morning I found my [?] traps gone & plenty of lobo trail—followed the drag & found a big lobo securely held by his front foot . . . He dragged the log (about 40 lb weight) 300 yards to the cañon of the creek—the nearest shelter, & then 150 yards down the creek in the water until the drag became caught in a low willow there . . . His companion had followed him as far as the creek.

"The other wolf who changed America—#672, Blanca—January 25, 1894," photograph by Seton. Philmont Museum.

There were at least three lessons to be learned from this. First, wolves have tremendous strength and stamina. Second, companion wolves stick together as much as possible. Third, terrible suffering is inflicted on living creatures by the use of steel traps. In his journal, Seton included his first sketch of a live wolf—a brutal scene capturing the wolf's panicked but defiant resistance to its own demise. Seton recorded no personal feelings about #653, but he was surprised by the wolf's resistance to the moment of its death. At a hundred pounds, it was the largest wolf he caught in New Mexico. Seton trapped two more wolves in December. One of them sheared a rope with its teeth when he tried to lasso it. He shot both at close range, the usual way of killing a trapped wolf. Each wolf was noted by a number in his journal. In the Lobo story, he noted, "Once or twice, I found indications that everything was not quite right in the Currumpaw pack. There were signs of irregularity, I thought; for instance there was clearly the trail of a smaller wolf running ahead of the leader, at times, and this I could not understand." A cowboy told him the tracks belonged to a white wolf, Blanca, Lobo's mate. If this were true, Seton realized, he might be able to overcome Lobo in a different way.

I killed a heifer and set one or two rather obvious traps about the carcass. Then cutting off the head, which is considered useless offal, and quite beneath the notice of a wolf, I set it a little

Right: "Blanca in her last moments," photograph by Seton, 1894. Philmont Museum.

Below: "Roping Gray Wolf," 1887. The cowboys shown here are strangling a wolf in the same way that Seton claimed to have strangled Blanca. Library of Congress.

No. 192 "Roping Gray Wolf."
Cow Boys take in a gray wolf on "Round Up."

apart and around it placed two powerful steel traps properly deodorized and concealed with the utmost care . . . The head was so placed that there was a narrow passage between it and some tussocks, and in this passage I buried two of my best traps, fastening them to the head itself.

Wolves have a habit of approaching every carcass they get the wind of, in order to examine it, even when they have no intention of eating of it, and I hoped that this habit would bring the Currumpaw pack within reach of my latest stratagem. I did not doubt that Lobo would detect my handiwork about the meat and prevent the pack approaching it, but I did build some hopes on the head, for it looked as though it had been thrown aside as useless.

Next morning, I sallied forth to inspect the traps, and there, oh joy! were the tracks of the pack, and the place where the beef-head and its traps had been was empty. A hasty study of the trail showed that Lobo had kept the pack from approaching the meat, but one, a small wolf, had evidently gone on to examine the head as it lay apart and had walked right into one of the traps.

Seton's journal gives a similar account of the trapping, although due to excitement or haste his always-sloppy handwriting is here nearly illegible.

Thursday 25 Jan. This a.m. I found the head of the beef in the pasture was gone—it had [?] *Allen and I follow the trail & found the white* [he added this word later] *wolf on a rock mesa 1½ miles away. I took 2 photos &* [?] *her but not before she had cut off both our ropes with her teeth. On level ground she could outrun a man through a* [?] *in the traps & the* [?] *with the two traps weighed 52 lbs. #672 Wolf ♀ weight 80 lbs. L. 5 ft 0½ in:* [?] *9½": Height at shoulder 25½." Chest 30 in She was very fat ♀ Blanca.* [This word added later.]

The journal entry does not specify Blanca's manner of death, but in the Lobo story Seton graphically describes a wolf-killing technique used at the time.

Then followed the inevitable tragedy, the idea of which I shrank from afterward more than at the time. We each threw a lasso over the neck of the doomed wolf, and strained our horses in opposite directions until the blood burst from her mouth, her eyes glazed, her limbs stiffened and then fell limp.

In his journal he continues:

Jan. 25 At night her mate came howling on the mesa—his calls repeated at intervals were most melancholy. Saw a lobo on the N. East mesa. [Followed by a wolf drawing.]

Jan. 26 The wolf of last night Lobo [a word he added later] *got caught in one trap—but managed to get out.*

Seton carried Blanca back to the ranch house, and from there dragged her body behind his horse, making wide arcs of scent trails. According to the story, he hoped to draw in the king wolf himself, believing that the bereft Lobo would come for her. On January 29 he caught another wolf, his fifth, although not the one he would call Lobo. He laid out more traps on the same day, claiming to have done so with particular cunning.

At length he [Lobo] *seemed to find the trail, and when he came to the spot where we had killed her, his heart-broken wailing was piteous to hear. It was sadder than I could possibly have believed. Even the stolid cowboys noticed it, and said they had "never heard a wolf carrying on like that before."*

After three months of continual effort, Seton was determined to make one more kill. On the cold morning of January 31 he went forth one last time.

It was afternoon of the next day before I got to the place referred to, and as I drew near a great grizzly form arose from the ground, vainly endeavoring to escape, and there revealed before me stood Lobo, King of the Currumpaw, firmly held in the traps. Poor old hero, he had never ceased to search for his darling, and when he found the trail her body had made he followed it recklessly, and so fell into the snare prepared for him. . . For two days and two nights he had lain there, and now was worn out with struggling. Yet, when I went near him, he rose up with bristling mane and raised his voice, and for the last time made the cañon reverberate with his deep bass roar, a call for help, the muster call of his band. But there was none to answer him . . .

The place where Lobo reputedly was captured—and photographed—is near an old barn where the current owners of the place can show you the exact spot where he was trapped. Seton does not explain it exactly that way in the story, seeming to suggest that the trap site was well away from any buildings—but perhaps these were built later. Seton put the still-living wolf across his saddle—likely to the extreme discomfort of his horse— and took Lobo back to the ranch, where he was staked out in an attempt to lure in more hapless members of the pack. In the story, Seton records the last moments of Lobo.

I set meat and water beside him, but he paid no heed. He lay calmly on his breast, and gazed with those steadfast yellow eyes away past me down through the gateway of the cañon, over

"Lobo in the four traps," photograph by Seton, January 31, 1894. Philmont Museum.

the open plains—his plains—nor moved a muscle when I touched him. When the sun went down he was still gazing fixedly across the prairie. I expected he would call up his band when night came, and prepared for them, but he had called once in his extremity, and none had come; he would never call again.

A lion shorn of his strength, an eagle robbed of his freedom, or a dove bereft of his mate, all die, it is said, of a broken heart; and who will aver that this grim bandit could bear the three-fold brunt, heart-whole? This only I know, that when the morning dawned, he was lying there still in his position of calm repose, his body unwounded, but his spirit was gone—the old King-wolf was dead.

Mammal specimen #677 was the last wolf ever caught by Ernest Thompson Seton. The date was January 31, 1894. He noted the event in his journal.

In morning at mouth of cañon—found a male ♂ lobo in traps—He was caught in 3 and had been in 4—he was unable to move at all—when I came near—he barked like a dog then broke into a prolonged howl—when Allen came—we tied his mouth shut & I carried him home—we staked him out for a decoy but he died in the evenng. **Why?**

Inflammation slight & apparently confined to toes. 677 Wolf ♂ Weight 78 lbs.

In the index to his Journal V, the daily record of his New Mexico adventure, Seton identified the wolf as "Lobo." What did he mean by "Why?" It must have been important because he wrote the question in dark ink, hard-pressed by his hand as he wrote it and in larger letters. Did he write that question on January 31, or at a later time? Did he mean to ask: Why did Lobo die after being captured? Or did he question what made him want to kill wolves? Or might he have asked the larger question of what makes humans act as the enemies of nature? Maybe all of these questions mattered to him, for he would work over several decades to find answers.

Conversion

Personal change can come out of the experience of trauma, such as that brought about by violent acts. The increasing level of violence Seton perpetrated against wildlife is nothing short of startling. New Mexico had proved an exceptionally bloody affair for him. Scores of animals had died by his hand—dogs, coyotes, wolves, badgers, skunks, rodents, and birds of many kinds. He did not write about his personal feelings afterward; he made no excuses for his behavior on the Currumpaw plains, nor did he ask pardon, but just as certainly, his life and attitudes were forever changed. The man he described in "The King of Currumpaw, A Wolf Story" was not the hero. Seton wrote the story to show that the only character with integrity was Lobo.

In its strongest form, the process of change takes on the form of conversion, which is often monumental in scope. It is defined by psychologist William James as the uniting of a previously divided self in a sudden or a gradual way. According to James, perhaps the strongest form of transformation occurs on a spiritual level:

We have a thought, or we perform an act, repeatedly, but on a certain day the real meaning of the thought peals through us for the first time, or the act has suddenly turned into a moral impossibility. All we know is that there are dead feelings, dead ideas and cold beliefs, and there are hot and live ones; and when one grows hot and alive within us, everything has to re-crystalize about it.

James goes on to explain that "Emotional occasions, especially violent ones, are extremely potent in precipitating mental rearrangements . . . emotions that come in this explosive way seldom leave things as they found them." These occasions occur in one of two ways, most dramatically by self-surrender, where a deep personal crisis finds sudden resolution, such as a near-instantaneous feeling of true connection to God. James calls the other occasion volitional, where "the regenerative change is usually gradual, and consists of the building up, piece by piece, of a new set of moral and spiritual habits. But there are always critical points here at which the movement forward seems much more rapid."

Seton could be put in the second category. He came to New Mexico with the goal of killing fifteen wolves, a number he might have reached had he remained. Instead, with the death of Lobo, the hunt came to a sudden end. On February 2 he returned to Clayton. The following day, he apparently collected $72 in state bounties for the six wolves. And on the next he "packed up" before sunrise and began the four-day train trip to Toronto. He claimed in his autobiography to have high-tailed it out of town on a midnight train, fleeing a false cattle-rustling charge, a story which clearly could not have been true given the time he spent in town before leaving. But it doesn't seem coincidental that he gave up wolf hunting the day of Lobo's death, despite his apparent plans to continue. Maybe he felt that he really was fleeing the scene of a crime.

Wolves kill for a reason; Seton had run out of reasons. On February 9, 1894, upon his return to Toronto, he wrote in his journal "End of Wolf Trip." It was a new beginning for the naturalist, who wrote Lobo's story over the next few weeks, quickly selling it to *Scribner's Magazine*. Lobo was an animal hero appearing in what may have been the first environmentalist literature, changing the way Americans looked at wildlife. At least some part of this change in perspective comes out of the process of naming. Nameless things can be killed with impunity, while a named character can receive our empathy. In the Lobo story, the author, as well as his readers, are transformed psychologically and politically as soon as they accept the wolf's change in identity from objective animal to subjective being. Killing animal #677 is one thing; killing "Lobo" is quite another.

In the decades following the publication of Lobo's story, the wolf became known to multitudes of children. In Seton's stories, animals are portrayed as personalities capable of making choices based on instinct, personal experience, and learning from others. In 1898, few scientists accepted the concept of animal wisdom. This new perception was critical because it meant that a living thing that can make specific decisions is, in some sense, sentient. While the broad scope of nature is amoral, the individual animal is conscious. Our human relationship to a sentient being must be different from a relationship that does not acknowledge consciousness and individuality. By Seton's reasoning, humans do not have the right to wantonly destroy animals and their habitats. Thoughtless destruction of life (arising in part from cowardice) is among the greatest acts of human immorality. Seton later used similar reasoning to criticize the white man's genocidal attacks on the American Indian, to criticize war and militarism in general, and to criticize the abusive educational system that separated youth from their own inherent nature as well as the natural world. Wild nature, Seton would argue, is necessary because it provides us with a standard for developing ourselves as moral individuals.

Seton came away from New Mexico with more than just blood on his hands. His contention that animals are related to humans in a moral sense would soon lead him to the logical conclusion that we are therefore responsible for their preservation. This is an example of his pervasive influence; while Seton's beliefs are axiomatic but nearly unknown to environmentalists today, the popularization of these concepts can be traced back to him more than anyone else.

Reviewing his New Mexico journal in 1917, Seton added a note about the importance of his time there. As usual in regard to matters of the greatest personal importance, he summarized: "This proved one of the turning points of my life for on my return I wrote Lobo."

CHAPTER TWO

Canada and Beyond

The early 1700s proved disastrous for many prominent Scottish families who supported the unsuccessful Jacobite rebellions, which aimed to restore the Stuart kings to the throne of Great Britain. Among the losers in the centuries-long contest with England were families named Cameron and Biddlestone, who lost everything in 1745, and another, the Setons, who had come to ruin earlier, in 1715. The Camerons fled Scotland to go into hiding—in northeastern England—under the assumed name of Thompson. The Thompsons prospered in England; in 1840, the fifth Cameron named Thompson—Joseph Logan Thompson—married Alice Snowdon. (A female Biddlestone had married a Snowdon, with that line carried on under the latter name.) One of Joseph and Alice's sons became Ernest Thompson Seton. (See Appendix 1: "Extended Note on Ancestry.")

The family lived in the gritty port town of South Shields on the River Tyne near Durham, where Ernest was born on August 14, 1860. The economy was based on coal and shipping; Joseph Thompson owned merchant ships, as had his father and father-in-law. Joseph's father, Enoch, denied his son's request to enter university as a civil engineer to take part in the new railroad fad. Enoch saw no future in railroads, betting the family legacy on wind-driven shipping. Joseph had limited interest in the business of managing his small fleet. In the 1860s, according to Ernest, his father had the same rotten luck as Antonio in *The Merchant of Venice*, losing four ships at sea within a short period of time: one ran aground in the Bristol Channel, one was seized by pirates off Guinea, another sank in the "Indian Seas," and a final one came to an unfortunate, unspecified end under a bad captain. Then a businessman whose notes Joseph had endorsed went broke. This scenario is not unlike the one in Shakespeare's play. Seton's version of his father's misfortune was probably a tongue-in-cheek reference to the bard; certainly it is the kind of literary joke Seton would have enjoyed. At the time of the disaster, whatever its details, Seton was five years old.

Seton chronicled his early years in two books, *Trail of an Artist-Naturalist* and *Two Little Savages*; all of his biographers

Right: Seton with his parents, ca. 1862. Philmont Museum.

Facing: *Self-portrait*, pen and ink, 1879. Drawn in London. Academy for the Love of Learning.

Self portrait. E.T Seton. 1879

have followed these closely. To read his account, much that he would become seemed at least foreshadowed, if not foreordained, before his birth. While pregnant with Ernest, his mother, Alice, went to the beach "clad in the preposterous, impossible, atrocious and perilous long bathing robe of that time." A sleeper wave knocked her down and nearly sucked her into the dangerous undertow. Reacting instantly, the family nurse grabbed Alice by her long hair and held on. Seton attributed his horror of the sea and all water to this incident. In any case, he was born prematurely, with thick, curly black hair, in contrast to his nine brothers, bald when newborn. Named Ernest Evan Thompson, he was the ninth of eleven children, and the eighth son. (Alice gave birth to one girl who died at age six and ten boys who survived.)

Ernest's middle name came from his ancestor Evan Cameron of Lochiel, a wolf hunter, and his first name from the title character of a now-forgotten novel, *Ernest Maltravers*, which Alice had read. Its author was Edward Bulwer-Lytton, whose novel *The Last Days of Pompeii* is still read and whose phrase "the great unwashed" is still spoken. Another of Bulwer-Lytton's novels begins with the line "It was a dark and stormy night," perhaps the most parodied phrase in the English language.

Of all his many brothers, Seton was the only writer and the only wolf hunter. As his first taste of hunting, he recalled spearing chickens and afterward feeling remorse. This too set a pattern for his future years, hunting at times, denouncing hunting at other times, and occasionally doing both at once.

Joseph and Alice Thompson (center), surrounded by their sons and a female cousin. Seton at back, center. Philmont Museum.

With the failure of his business, Joseph Thompson made the momentous decision to leave England. Seton was not yet six when his family embarked on the great voyage to Canada. He carried his few belongings in a small wooden case still owned by his family today. He afterward also carried with him unusually vivid memories for one so young, recording in his autobiography, "I see yet the piles and piles of boxes all lashed with strong, tarry rope that told of the ship tradition. I can still smell the cats in that cheap lodging in Glasgow where we spent a day and a night before going aboard the *St. Patrick*, a steamer bound for Quebec." He recalled as well the shipboard rats and the sour bread he ate at the hotel where they stayed in Quebec. Less clear was what followed—a long trip into interior Canada, where his father had decided to become a farmer outside the barely existent town of Lindsay, Ontario. Ernest recounted that his father was temperamentally ill-equipped for the harsh physical life of the prairie farmer. He criticized the old man for his presumptions. Having read *The Swiss Family Robinson* and *Robinson Crusoe*, Joseph—according to his son—believed himself ready for the challenge: "Father came prepared for the life of an English country gentleman. He proposed to take a huge track of virgin forest, with a lake in it, build a castle on the lake, and live the life; so brought his library, his scientific instruments, and a dozen different sporting guns." A long time later, in Connecticut, Seton would reclaim a second-growth forest, create a lake, build a castle beside it, and fill that castle with his scientific equipment, library, rifles, and one wolf pelt. Apparently, he couldn't resist a

The Elms, Lindsay, Ontario, was the early residence of the Seton family in Canada, n.d. Library and Archives Canada.

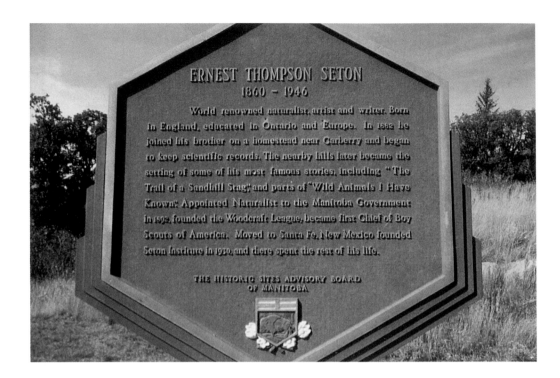

ERNEST THOMPSON SETON
1860 – 1946

World renowned naturalist, artist and writer. Born in England, educated in Ontario and Europe. In 1882 he joined his brother on a homestead near Carberry and began to keep scientific records. The nearby hills later became the setting of some of his most famous stories, including "The Trail of a Sandhill Stag" and parts of "Wild Animals I Have Known." Appointed Naturalist to the Manitoba Government in 1892, founded the Woodcraft League, became first Chief of Boy Scouts of America. Moved to Santa Fe, New Mexico founded Seton Institute in 1930, and there spent the rest of his life.

THE HISTORIC SITES ADVISORY BOARD
OF MANITOBA

"Most boys gather in the woods pretty and odd bits of moss, fungus, and other treasures that have no price. They bring them home and store them in that universal receptacle, the Tackle-box. Some boys, like myself, never outgrow the habit. One day a friend observed that my Tackle-box was full and suggested that a selection be given to the public."
—Woodmyth and Fable

metaphorical poke in the eye at his unsuccessful father, notwithstanding the old man's death years before.

Whatever his father's failures, life in the country in Canada suited young Ernest perfectly. It was here that he lighted his first campfire and recalled "the sweet and holy fragrance of the balsam trees about us." He remembered also the scent of a slaughtered deer, his revulsion at the ax murder of a groundhog by farmers, and the reading of a story about the grief of a mother polar bear at the killing of her cubs by hunters. He reacted with a "choking sorrow"; yet soon he became a hunter himself. His sixteen-year-old teacher, Agnes O'Leary, introduced him to the bear story. Decades later he would inscribe a copy of *Two Little Savages* to her who "taught me to read and write in a little log cabin in Lindsay, Ont."

Reading would prove one of the two salvations of Seton's early life. The other saving grace was woodcraft, a set of outdoor skills and knowledge central to Seton's story.

Woodcraft included nature study, outdoor skills for self-sufficiency, and "Indian lore." Like John Muir a generation earlier, Ernest and the kids of Lindsay had to make much of what they used in their lives. A capacity for invention was a particularly useful attribute. He learned to use every kind of knife, ax, saw, and basic carpentry tool to construct everything from furniture to buildings. From his more experienced neighbors he discovered the uses of every tree that grew in the area: white hickory made a good ax handle; blue beech could be shredded for brooms; "cedar" (juniper) proved exceptionally good for starting fires. Two large trees on the family homestead gave the place its name, The Elms. Trees and wood mattered a great deal to Seton, and he would later write a forestry manual. He lived an idyllic frontier life at The Elms, but after four years his father had to admit failure once more. The older sons had moved on to more promising ventures as soon as they could get away. For Joseph, now in his fifties, this meant starting over yet again. He left farming for accounting, a profession at which he was more able. He moved his remaining family to a rough neighborhood in a poor district of Toronto, where Ernest's crossed eyes and slim build made him "Squinty" to the local bullies. He was in enough fights to have earned a nose disfigurement not fully repaired until an operation in the 1920s. Many an opponent learned that despite his small size, he didn't shy from a fight, a character trait he never outgrew.

Above: Seton at age fourteen. Philmont Museum.

Facing: Seton Wayside Park, Carberry, Manitoba, 2007. Seton lived near this small Canadian town during the 1880s. Photo credit: Bill Taylor.

Another aspect of Seton's courage was his love of adventure and exploration, particularly his fascination with birds. The young Ernest burned with a passion to know the names and habits of every feathered creature he saw. At thirteen he struggled to come up with the one dollar needed to purchase *Birds of Canada*, apparently the first book of its kind. As sometimes happens, the prize did not live up to expectations, and he experienced considerable frustration in trying to master avian taxonomy. In typical Seton fashion, he would not give up until he mastered the subject, eventually writing a *Key to the Birds of Canada*, a technical guide to identification of bird families, and *Birds of Manitoba*, his first attempt at substantial nature writing. In the meantime, he began exploring the Don River Valley and its marsh on the shores of Lake Ontario, mostly alone, starting from the time he was around twelve. The experience of discovery made him ecstatic, as he noted in his autobiography: "The joy Balboa had in discovering the Pacific, or La Salle the Mississippi, could not possibly have been deeper, purer, higher, than what I had in finding and exploring this great, glorious wilderness. It was mine! I felt by right of discovery."

He named his personal woodland on the Don River "Glenyan," later giving the name "Yan" to his alter ego in *Two Little Savages*. Glenyan took center stage in his life; he disappeared into its reaches at every opportunity. When he was fourteen, he built a tiny cabin, or "shanty," as he called it, out of found materials worked with the simplest of tools. On-site he made for himself a bow, arrows, moccasins, and birch bark containers so that he could emulate what he thought the life of traditional Indians might have been like. He even exposed himself from the waist up to create sunburn that would turn him red. The idyll ended when a group of "tramps" moved into the place and defiled it. The adventure of doing this, however, combined his love of nature, crafts, and Indian culture. Here at Glenyan he established guiding principles that would occupy him for a lifetime. Many of the basic ideas for Woodcraft and the Boy Scouts came directly from this early experience. In *Two Little Savages*, *The Book of Woodcraft*, and elsewhere, he described the physical accomplishments made possible by living close to the land; but these accomplishments also occupied a deeper psychological space. He wrote of himself as a boy in *Two Little Savages*:

> *His heart was more and more in his kingdom now; he longed to come and live here. But he only dared to dream that some day he might be allowed to pass a night in the shanty. This was where he would lead his ideal life—the life of the Indian with all that is bad and cruel left out. Here he would show men how to live without cutting down all the trees, spoiling all the streams, and killing every living thing. He would learn how to get the dullest pleasure out of the woods himself and then teach others how to do the same. Though the birds and the Fourfoots fascinated him, he would not have hesitated to shoot one had he been able; but to see a tree cut down always caused him the greatest distress. Possibly he realized that the bird might be quickly replaced, but the tree, never.*

Although Seton was devastated by the loss of his little cabin, spending the summer of his fifteenth year in Lindsay with the family that had purchased his father's farm restored his spirits. He returned to farm chores and, showing his natural leadership ability, invented games to share with other children. During the next summer in Lindsay, seriously ill with malaria, using only a fish spear, he fought off and mortally wounded a hungry mother lynx that had invaded his new cabin. In September 1876, he added one more item to his list of major interests. While he had previously made drawings and even prints, and had taken a few lessons in oil painting, for the first time the idea that he might become an artist opened up for him. Walking in the Don Valley, he found a sharp-shinned hawk dead in the weeds. He devised a frame to hold the

bird in a flying position and spent two weeks attempting to paint the image. The result was a remarkable first painting that captured the hawk in considerable detail, from its individual feathers to the broader pattern of the underside of its wings. His father immediately recognized his son's considerable natural talent and the possibility of his having a career as an illustrator.

Seton soon took up an apprenticeship of sorts with a minor portrait painter. More importantly, he enrolled at the Ontario School of Art, where he soon came to the attention of two women who took an interest in his career. Both were wealthy and became his earliest patrons. One was the realist painter and Royal Canadian Academy of Arts member Charlotte Schreiber. He spent time working in a studio at her estate and apparently looked up to her. The other was Toronto socialite Anne Arthurs, who was well known for her support of charitable organizations. A Toronto historian wrote:

Sharp-shinned Hawk, oil on canvas on paperboard, 1876. This is Seton's first painting. Academy for the Love of Learning. Photo credit: James Hart.

Anne Arthurs was always quick to recognize and encourage artistic talent in the young. . . . Among them was the artist-naturalist Ernest Thompson Seton who was a familiar visitor at Ravenswood [Anne Arthurs's house] *in the closing years of the nineteenth century. . . . He usually approached Ravenswood along the private drive that curved across the Spadina* [nearby mansion; Indian word for "hill"] *lawn from the west, and was always recognized by his swinging gait and mass of black hair that curled beneath his broad-brimmed hat. Attracted by the flight or call of a bird, he would often check his stride, and standing motionless, observe it with prolonged concentration.*

Arthurs would continue her patronage into the future, purchasing from Seton a few years later a copy of an oil painting by Sir Edwin Landseer, an English wildlife artist who painted scenes of heroic animals and whose stylistic influence was then still strong in England.

American and Canadian painters of this period faced an important problem in their art training. With a few exceptions, North American painting teachers had not achieved the same level of practice as their European counterparts. And many of the best American painters lived in France on a part- or full-time basis. Every serious art student reached a moment when he or she had learned all they could from local talent. To progress in their studies, a trip abroad became inevitable. Most students went to Paris, or to Germany or Italy, often as side trips from Paris. Because he was a British subject, and possibly because he had relatives in the area, Seton decided to study in London.

Armed with little knowledge of the world and a miserly loan from his father, he left for England in June 1879, intending to study at the Royal Academy. The competition to get into this institution was perhaps greater than he expected—he was rejected in his first attempt. In his second try, he not only got in, but was also awarded a scholarship to pay his tuition beginning in January 1881. His interest in taking formal classes was probably limited. He followed the common practice of that time of sketching great works of art in museums and completing the work at home or in a studio. He also constantly sketched from live specimens at the zoo. He spent hours painting in art studios. He continually studied at the library of the British Museum after getting a lifetime pass by writing letters, he said, to the Archbishop of Canterbury and the Prince of Wales. Special permission was needed for a nineteen-year-old to even get through the door. Apparently, his powers of persuasion were already well honed. Once there, he became familiar with the writings of Henry David Thoreau, John Burroughs, and other naturalists.

Seton's Royal Academy token, front and back, 1881. Philmont Museum.

Left: *Fox and Goats,* oil on canvas, 1881. Academy for the Love of Learning. Photo credit: James Hart.

Below: Head study, pencil, possibly drawn at the Art Students League in 1883. Academy for the Love of Learning.

When not working he walked for hours, despite a severe hernia and the heavy truss he wore to deal with it. He took the occasional odd job making illustrations and showed his work at a local art gallery but didn't sell anything. Having almost no money, he ate very little. Seton, at six feet, was taller than average for the time, but also quite thin, and in failing health. Working eighteen hours a day and eating very little was a habit he would continue for many years. (He may have suffered from malnutrition and continuing aftereffects of malaria.) Artwork that he completed at this time included *Fox and Goats*, depicting an animal hero—a mother goat defending her kid from a fox—set against an idyllic landscape including a cabin with smoking chimney. He also created an exceptionally romantic self-portrait in ink and many drawings of animals from life. His artistic output was prodigious, and the pace he set for himself impossible to maintain. Yet in the midst of the frenetic activity, he clearly found time for reflection, writing "The Plan of My Life," which he kept among his papers until the day he died.

Below: *Lion Portrait,* charcoal, 1879. Drawn in London. Academy for the Love of Learning.

Facing: *Lion's Head,* pen and ink, 1880. Drawn in London. Academy for the Love of Learning.

I, Ernest Evan, eighth son of Joseph Logan Thompson, whose right surname is Seton, and who is the sole and lawful heir of George Seton, Earl of Winton, being of sound mind though not of robust body, do hereby outline and forecast my own life in the light of knowledge of myself and my surroundings.

This coming spring, I shall exhibit a picture at the Royal Academy Exhibition.

I shall return to Canada for the winter, I shall there undergo a dangerous operation for the radical cure of the rupture that now distresses me and shall be perfectly and happily cured. This I shall undertake against the advice of all my friends.

On my 21st birthday I shall pubickly [sic] resume our proper family name of Seton, and thenceforth be known as Ernest E. T. Seton. In doing this I shall have trouble chiefly with my own people.

I shall spend a year in writing and illustrating a book on The Birds of Canada, with Jos. Mc. P. Ross. The book will give me great pleasure, it will make for me a local reputation and will bring me some money.

I shall then go to New York to make my way as an illustrator and painter of animals.

In 1890 I shall marry an English woman, or of English extraction; she will have light hair and blue eyes, be of medium or small size, inclined to be stout. That is, in all ways the reverse of myself. Mentally she shall fill the gaps where I fail. God grant I may know her when she comes, that I waste no time on following others.

"*It was that pioneer, Ernest Thompson Seton, who first tried the idea of pattern diagrams as a method of teaching bird identification. . . . It was on this idea that my Field Guide to the Birds, the Eastern counterpart of this volume, was based.*"
—Roger Tory Peterson, *A Field Guide to Western Birds*

Above: *Juncos*, ink and gouache, 1881. Academy for the Love of Learning.

Right: *Solomon Seal & Veery*, ink wash and pencil, 1881. Academy for the Love of Learning.

We shall have three children, two boys and a girl. The first boy will be a source of sorrow, but in the other two we shall find much happiness.

In 1905 I shall by God's help, have made a comfortable fortune by my pen and pencil also by judicious speculation. I shall then return to England, buy a small estate in Devonshire, and a house in London.

In 1915 I shall be knighted by the King in recognition of my work as an artist naturalist.

In 1924, I shall die in my London home, of a bronchial trouble, during the spring of the year, being then in my 64th year.

This is my destiny to restore in a measure the ancient Family name of Seton, of which my father is the rightful representative. And whensoever I shall turn aside from this plan I shall have great trouble. And such deviations will always be brought about by the active interference of my immediate family, therefore to be safe I should avoid them.

Nevertheless my heart cleaves to my own people.

Overall, Seton's record of accomplishment in relation to this list turned out rather well. He did undergo a modern procedure to treat the hernia that resulted in a lengthy convalescence, but also a complete cure. He did end up illustrating and contributing to bird books for J. H. Stickney, Ralph Hoffmann, and Frank M. Chapman, as well as a short one of his own. He did marry, twice, resulting in one biological daughter of his first marriage and one adopted daughter of his second. His first wife was American of English extraction, had blonde hair and blue eyes, and was rather small. Both of his wives did complement him in important ways. By 1905 he had made a fortune by his pen and pencil. He was never knighted but did become Chief Scout of the Boy Scouts of America, a more singular and important honor. He died not as an ailing man in 1924 but as an old one in 1946. He continued to obsess over the name of Seton, right through the writing of his autobiography in the late 1930s.

By October 1881, exhausted and perhaps simply overwhelmed by his passion to absorb everything there was to know about whatever interested him, his experiment with art school came to an end. And with it came, for now, an end to whatever interest he had in city life. Throughout his life, the call of the West, whether in the United States or Canada, would grow ever stronger until, in later years, his increasingly frequent visits would lead him to full-time residency. Later he would call this urge the Buffalo Wind.

Seton returned home to Canada, where he received his first major illustration commission: Christmas cards featuring birds of Toronto. With the proceeds, he bought chickens and headed west by train—through one of the worst blizzards ever recorded in

Right: *M. subulatus* (bat), ink, 1887. Academy for the Love of Learning.

Below: *Big-billed Water Thrush*, ink, ca. 1885. Academy for the Love of Learning.

the central region of North America. He nearly starved on the train as a three-day trip turned into one lasting over two weeks. He survived on raw chicken eggs. Along the way he saw an encounter among animals he would later turn into a short story. As the train moved slowly through the snowbound world, Seton looked out to see a circle of dogs surrounding a huge lone wolf. As the dogs attacked singly or in groups, the wolf defended itself, killing some of the attackers. The train moved on, but he found out later that the wolf had survived to experience further adventures. These he recorded in "The Winnipeg Wolf."

> *Wolf? He looked like a lion. There he stood, all alone—resolute—calm—with bristling mane, and legs braced firmly, glancing this way and that, to be ready for an attack in any direction. . . . How I wished for the train to stick in a snowdrift now, as so often before, for all my heart went out to the Gray-wolf; I longed to go and help him.*

Seton imagined what would make a wolf choose to live alone and in proximity to people. In his story, a bounty hunter murders a wolf family; a surviving pup is raised and abused by humans who force it to fight dogs. The wolf's only friend and companion is a boy, who dies. After the boy's death, the wolf escapes but stays near the cemetery where he is buried. The wolf is finally hunted down and killed by men and dogs—defiant to the last. There is no shame in his heroic defeat but great shame on those who have persecuted him.

Having seen the magnificent wolf and survived the grueling train passage, Seton began a new phase of his life in and around Carberry, Manitoba, "The Land of My Dreams," as he titled it in *Trail of an Artist-Naturalist*. Over the next eighteen months he gradually sold off his sixty chickens—plus eggs—for a considerable profit. This enabled him to spend nearly as much time as he wanted exploring the conifer-covered sandhills along the Assiniboine River and its tributaries in the southern part of the province. It was out of his experiences of this time that he would develop his great hunting story "The Trail of the Sandhill Stag," about his ongoing search for and ultimately nonviolent encounter with a deer. He filed a claim on homestead land that he would abandon and to which he never would return. He marveled at the bird life and began developing his ideas for identifying birds on the wing, even over considerable distances. He removed and counted the feathers of a Brewer's grackle, finding that it had 4,915. He began a correspondence with ornithologists at the Smithsonian Institution in Washington, D.C., which would soon result in important friendships and career-building connections. Canadian mammals equally fascinated Seton. Liberated from his rupture-supporting truss after the successful operation in 1882, he now seemed to have unlimited energy. He

Above left: *Clay Sparrow*, watercolor and ink, 1882. Academy for the Love of Learning.

Above right: *Coots and Their Nest*, ink, 1881. Academy for the Love of Learning.

studied animal tracks in the snow, learning to distinguish the exact sequence of complex animal interactions. He was the first or among the first to discover the importance of musk-scent marking by wolves as a means of informing other wolves of "the personality, sex, condition, and emotions of the one who left the record."

He interrupted this idyll for a few months during the winter of 1883–84 to visit New York City, arriving as usual in a new place with no money and without knowing anyone. By the time he left five months later he had made many new friends and come into contact with influential people who would be helpful to him in the future. He obtained a well-paying job as an illustrator and attended the Art Students League, where, then as now, artists work intensely, often becoming superb draftsmen. Perhaps most importantly, he began writing animal stories. Then, typically, he dropped everything and returned to Carberry, where he could study birds and hunt big game. He figured that New York could wait on him until he felt like resuming his place there.

The Buffalo Wind had called him west once more. He spent a pleasant summer roaming about and building a cabin he didn't need on land he claimed but had no interest in. In late October, he and a companion tracked a deer they had shot and wounded. They found the deer but so had a "Fenimore Cooper Indian," a man of striking and, to Seton, wonderful appearance, like someone out of one of the old novels.

He was a Cree named Chaska. He was about six feet tall in his moccasins, straight and well built, his features decidedly aquiline. His hair hung in two long black braids, ornamented with

a bunch of brass rings and thimbles. A scarlet handkerchief covered his ears. He carried the usual fire-bag, knife and gun. He was a minor chief, and evidently a man of experience, for he spoke excellent English.

We took to each other from the beginning. There was an indefinable charm about his quiet dignified manners—and I knew that he could teach me much about woodcraft.

Chaska was a brilliant woodsman from whom Seton learned new lessons in animal tracking over several weeks until they parted, never to meet again. Chaska would make a brief appearance in Seton's 1899 story "The Trail of the Sandhill Stag," and over twenty years after that story was published, Seton would honor his friend by using his name for an Indian character in a novel, *The Preacher of Cedar Mountain*. Seton also honored his friend by naming a small lake near Carberry "Chaska-Water" and creating a series of drawings depicting the place and its connection to the First Nation's peoples. The lake had long been a haven for waterfowl, but by the 1920s, when Seton returned, it had become a dry, sandy grassland used by local farmers as a hay meadow. A spruce forest now encroaches on the field and a gravel road has been laid across a portion of it. In his autobiography, Seton decried the loss of natural wetlands:

Gone are the ducks and geese, the muskrats and mink, the myriad wild fowl, swallows and tern, snipe and rails, coots and bittern. Gone with the drying of the land, for on the whole Northwest the selfsame blight is cast. Ten thousand little lakes are gone, dried up, a wholesale

Above left: *Prairie Chickens,* ink and gouache, ca. 1880s. Academy for the Love of Learning.

Above right: *Domestic Birds,* ink with pencil, ca. 1880s. Academy for the Love of Learning.

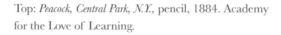

Top: *Peacock, Central Park, N.Y.*, pencil, 1884. Academy for the Love of Learning.

Bottom left: *Pintail*, oil on illustration board, ca. 1880s. Academy for the Love of Learning.

Bottom right: *The Sea Ducks*, ink wash and gouache, 1883. Academy for the Love of Learning.

Top: *Mother Panther*, pen and ink, 1885. Academy for the Love of Learning.

Bottom left: *Cougar*, ink, ink wash, and gouache, ca. 1880s–1890s. Academy for the Love of Learning.

Bottom right: *Mule Deer*, watercolor, 1889. Philmont Museum.

Top: *Song Sparrow*, ink wash and gouache, 1885. Academy for the Love of Learning.

Bottom: *Bob White*, gouache over printed image, 1890. Academy for the Love of Learning.

desiccation of the land begun, the wholesale wiping out of myriad marshes and lakes, the homeland of the wild and wet-foot. It seems to please the farmers; for much rich land is thereby made available. And so long as there is rain, they fear no drought. But alas, it means the destruction of thousands of bird haunts, it lessens the bird hosts by millions each year; and when we seek to explain our "Vanishing Wild Life," we must not overlook the fact that one element in the problem is the ending of the countless ponds and lakelets in the far Northwest.

He had one last adventure in Carberry, shortly after leaving his friend Chaska. He hunted a moose as relentlessly as Yan hunts the deer in "Trail of the Sandhill Stag." But in this case, Seton killed the great animal, claiming remorse afterward. He wrote that he never again killed any large game animals. But it is more accurate to say that he never killed another moose, although he would later help his first wife, Grace, to kill one. Seton was sorry later that he had not claimed land along the shores of Chaska-Water, but he had other plans at the time. He didn't say if there was an anti-Buffalo Wind, but perhaps there was, for the call of the East was, in its way, as powerful as that of the West. He was driven to make his art and writing on natural history count for something important in the world.

For the remainder of the 1880s, he divided most of his time between Toronto and New York, pursuing major illustration assignments—including one to provide a thousand illustrations for *The Century Dictionary*. Nearing thirty, he must have decided he should settle down into something. He published a major paper with the Smithsonian, *Birds of Manitoba*, but it was not his best work, and he knew it.

After spending some time caretaking a resort for one of his brothers, in the summer of 1890 Seton left again for London for more sketching at the zoo, but within a few months he would at last go on to Paris for additional art training. At that time, it was common for illustrators to study painting in Paris, even those already in their late twenties and early thirties. Such a long apprenticeship would be unusual now. Still, there were worse things than to be an unmarried artist living in Paris in 1891. Like other foreigners, he entered Académie Julian, not the most prestigious place, but one where North Americans—or at least their tuition fees—were gladly accepted. Nude models, the French language, leftist politics, and rising stars like the later well-known artist Robert Henri were all part of the milieu in which Seton found himself.

At the time, the goal of all art students, as well as professional artists, was acceptance of one or more paintings into the Salon. The oncoming Modernist revolution would soon make the Salon itself seem no more than a quaint nineteenth-century habit, but at the time it was important enough that Seton took the competition seriously. His subject, of course, was a wolf. And the painting he produced, *The Sleeping Wolf*, is probably the finest he produced in his entire career. The model lived at the Ménagerie du Jardin des Plantes and was in the habit of taking a sunlit nap in the same spot on a regular basis. The impatient Seton probably preferred drawing because working with pen and pencil was much faster than working with slow-drying oils; he could produce much more work in graphic mediums. The Salon accepted drawings, but the top honor for an artist was acceptance of an oil painting. Seton wrote that the work took a full month at several hours per day, a claim easily believed by the detail he captured. Everything we might consider noble and beautiful about a wild animal comes through in this painting. The setting is so beautiful that we feel as if we have come upon this animal in a state of total peace in a remote woodland. The truth of the wolf's situation was of course different, but the illumination surrounding the animal makes us believe that nature has created a special light just for this wolf in this moment.

The Salon accepted the painting and even hung it in a favorable spot—a distinction not always given to the few Americans and Canadians lucky enough to get into the show. (The French were generally correct in their assessment of the Americans and Canadians as presenting no more than modest talent.) Although he does not say so,

Top left: *Muskrat*, mixed media, 1892. Academy for the Love of Learning.

Top right and bottom: *Two English Sparrows*, ink and pencil and gouache, 1880. Academy for the Love of Learning.

Right: *The Rooky Woods*, watercolor, 1891. Philmont Museum.

Facing, top: *Landscape with Water*, watercolor, 1891. Painted in Paris. Academy for the Love of Learning.

Facing, bottom: *Landscape with Reflecting Pool*, watercolor, 1891. Academy for the Love of Learning.

Right: Untitled forest scene #1, ink and pencil, 1888. Academy for the Love of Learning.

Below: Untitled forest scene, ink, ca. 1890s. Academy for the Love of Learning.

Facing: *Shrike,* watercolor, ink, and gouache, 1890. Academy for the Love of Learning.

Above: *The Hermitage*, pen and ink and ink wash, ca. 1890. Academy for the Love of Learning.

Top left: Standing nude female, charcoal, 1891. Academy for the Love of Learning.

Bottom left: Standing nude male, charcoal, 1891. Academy for the Love of Learning.

Left: *Landscape with Trees*, watercolor, 1891. Painted in France. Academy for the Love of Learning.

Below: Dog study, watercolor, 1891. Philmont Museum.

The Sleeping Wolf, oil on canvas on plywood, 1891. Academy for the Love of Learning. Photo credit: James Hart.

Seton sold the painting, probably in 1895, and perhaps for as much as a thousand dollars (roughly $25,000 now). If it sold for anywhere near that amount, his willingness to part from it is understandable. He never saw it again during his lifetime; it was lost to the knowledge of the Seton family until it turned up again in the 1960s. The family scrambled to raise the money needed to buy it back so that it could be displayed at Seton Castle in Santa Fe.

Seton's confidence was bolstered by this important success. He decided to create an even more impressive work for the Salon of the following year. After reading about a French wolf hunter killed by vengeful wolves, he decided to make a scene of the aftermath of the killing—*Triumph of the Wolves.* Painting this time on a much larger canvas, he worked outside in a park, setting up human remains and using animal blood as props. He claimed to have been arrested by the police on suspicion of murder;

Triumph of the Wolves (aka *Awaited in Vain*), oil on canvas, 1892. Painted in Paris. A pack of wolves has taken revenge on a French wolf hunter, killing and devouring him within sight of his own house. Philmont Museum. Photo credit: Dave Emery.

certainly if the police did happen upon a crazed artist surrounded by bones and blood, they would have had legitimate reason to ask probing questions. (He also sketched dead dogs in a serious effort to understand canine anatomy.) To move the focus from the wolves to the humans, he renamed the painting *Awaited in Vain* (*La Vaine Attente*), an unintentionally appropriate title. The Salon jury hated the painting and its message of nature triumphing over man. Or maybe they just found it ugly and revolting. The conservative Salon had a bias against the unconventional, and this painting clearly broke the rules.

Upset by this rejection, Seton returned home with the painting, hoping to get it into the World's Columbian Exposition (the Chicago World's Fair) of 1893. When he failed at this, he launched an ill-considered letter-writing campaign in the spring and enlisted one or more friendly politicians on his side as well. When his attempts at reconsideration got nowhere, he redoubled his efforts and finally made such a pest of himself that the painting was included in the Canadian pavilion at the exposition. But as a final insult to him, the irritated organizers may have "skyed" the painting; that is, they may have hung it on a high dark wall where it could not be seen.

Similar, although less dramatic, persistence on Seton's part got him the title of Naturalist for the Province of Manitoba in 1892. Like his success in finally showing

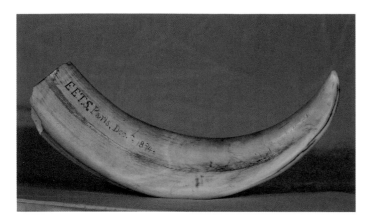

Incised boar tusk
(E.E.T.S.), Paris, 1894.
Academy for the Love
of Learning.

Awaited in Vain, this recognition didn't change his life very much. These two events must have been on Seton's mind when he decided to go wolf hunting in New Mexico. As well, a third factor may have played into his decision: one of his American friends from Paris, Irving Couse, was attempting just such a career move, and would do so successfully, later becoming one of the best-known members of the Taos, New Mexico, art colony. At thirty-two, Seton had not yet made it as an artist—he was, and would remain, in his own words, an illustrator. He was not ready to give up just yet, but he needed to get away from the embarrassments *Awaited in Vain* had caused him. He would come back to New York some years later as a champion of lost causes with his leadership of the Woodcraft movement. In the meantime, he would try his hand at being a wolf hunter.

CHAPTER THREE

The Foundations of Wildlife Conservation

S eton nearly missed the boat to Paris. The last passenger to arrive on the SS *Spaarndam*, he leapt from dock to ship, since the gangplank had already been pulled in. A small leap, but, as it turns out, an important one. When the ship set out for France in July 1894, Seton had finished up his business with Fitz Randolph; Lobo would not make his appearance in print for another four months.

Seton developed a shipboard interest in twenty-two-year-old Grace Gallatin, the daughter of a wealthy California family, traveling with her mother. They pursued a romance in Paris and married in New York two years later. In his usual manner, Seton found plenty of other projects to keep him busy in France, starting with the creation of his first real book. His earlier effort, a monograph on the birds of Manitoba, had been a flop; in his hurry to produce something, he had issued a poorly conceived work. But he had learned from this mistake, taking plenty of time to put together the innovative *Studies in the Art Anatomy of Animals*, a guidebook to the musculature and bone structure of animals (including canines) with well-thought-out text and magnificent technical drawings. At the time, there was nothing like it, and well over a century later, the book is still in print.

Simultaneously, Seton painted a new entry for the 1895 Salon. With *The Pursuit* (*La Poursuite*), he finished his trilogy of major wolf paintings. This time he depicted a running wolf pack chasing a sleigh through dark, snowy woods. Ten ferocious wolves, fangs flashing, eyes wide in excitement, charge into the scene. The viewer's breathtaking perspective is an over-the-shoulder glance back at the pursuers, although neither sleigh nor person makes an appearance. The painting is a *tour de force* of wolf anatomy with sinister implication. This is not the docile *Sleeping Wolf* of nature at peace; this is nature at war—and we are the target. The Salon judges decided to show Seton's individual wolf-study sketches for the

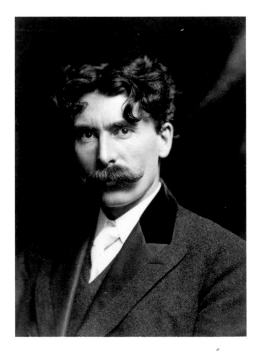

Ernest Thompson Seton, ca. 1910. Library of Congress.

painting but rejected the oil itself from the annual exhibition. *The Pursuit* and *Awaited in Vain* are now in the collection of the Philmont Museum, where the wolves still glower out at the viewer over a century after they were first painted.

With this rejection by the ultra-conservative Salon, Seton came to realize that the success he sought would have to come from another direction than through painting. He was disappointed but not crushed. Rejection from one avenue meant entry into some other. Although he had arrived in Paris with almost no money, he brimmed with confidence and ideas. He later had one of his personal notes typed up.

December 22, 1894

> *I have spent all the afternoon at the Louvre and as I went from one great master to another and saw all kinds of peculiarities and extremes yet all resulting in great pictures—there was one lesson that was impressed on me more and more—the man who does immortal work develops himself.*
>
> *Here have I, living in Norway, been trying to grow a palm tree because I saw that African palms were good. And each fresh frost cut down my puny sprout. It has only recently dawned on me that I must grow my pine. It is the timber of my soil. What a noble tree I might have had now had I realized this ten years ago.*
>
> *This then is my theory: I have something which no one else in the world has. It may be a little thing, but it is me. It is my pine tree and I shall grow it, though it never exceed a foot in height. It will at least be a living thing.*

Grace Gallatin Seton, after 1905. Library of Congress.

Seton and Grace returned to the United States in April 1896, sending out announcements of their engagement and scheduling the wedding for October. Instead, without comment, the wedding was suddenly moved up to June. The usual reason for rushing ahead with a wedding did not appear; Grace did not give birth to her only child, Ann, until more than seven years later. Mr. and Mrs. Seton-Thompson took up residence on a country estate—Sloat Hall—in New Jersey and, soon, in a Manhattan apartment as well, continuing the country/city dichotomy that would define their lives. In his typical fashion, Seton recorded the fact of his marriage with one rather terse entry in his journal: "June 1st—Married Grace Gallatin. Presb church NY." Following this, he recorded an extensive list of birds he had identified on his new property.

Grace loved the city but was willing to learn about the wilderness from her husband. Seton loved the wilderness but found city life much more tolerable with his

The Pursuit, oil on canvas, 1895. Painted in Paris. Philmont Museum. Photo credit: Dave Emery.

loving companion. He took on illustration assignments for important bird field guides, contributing his own identification scheme and categorization of bird families, as well as publishing more animal stories. He began to get noticed for his art and writing, and also for his storytelling ability. In mid-November he told wolf stories to a small literary group that included Theodore Roosevelt. The future president invited Seton to tell more stories at the Boone and Crockett Club annual dinner. Seton did more than recite stories to the elite hunters' group; he also did sound effects, making all the bird and mammal calls appropriate to the story. His wolf howl made a particularly strong impression on his listeners, some of whom began referring to him as "Wolf Thompson." Given his rise in the arts and the literary world, Seton did not wish to take the chance of abandoning New York; nonetheless, summers in the East held little appeal to him. In her first book, Grace wrote her version of what happened next:

So when, the year after our marriage, Nimrod announced that the mountain madness was again working in his blood, and that he must go West and take up the trail for his holiday, I tucked my summer-watering-place-and-Europe-flying-trip mind away (not without regret, I confess) and cautiously tried to acquire a new vocabulary and some new ideas.

Grace soon overcame her reluctance and took to wilderness exploration and hunting with an enthusiasm that must have delighted her husband. The summer of 1897 saw them off to Yellowstone National Park, where Seton entered the next phase of his conversion from wildlife hunter to wildlife protector. He fell in love with Yellowstone and its wildlife, although not its boiling mud springs and geysers. (He enjoyed the scenery but his passion went out almost exclusively to those aspects of nature that were furred or feathered.) A few years later he included stories about Yellowstone in *Lives of the Hunted* and *Wild Animals at Home*, while Grace wrote her account of their Western adventures during their first two years together in *A Woman Tenderfoot*, published in 1900.

The Yellowstone trip came about because of the Camp Fire Club, newly formed by one of the earliest wildlife conservationists, William T. Hornaday, with support from Seton, Dan Beard, and others. The club developed a woodsy recreational site for its members—a kind of refuge for New York urbanites to escape to on weekends. It also published a magazine, *Recreation*, in which Seton published much of his early work. The following year he wrote enthusiastically in his articles about predators and prey, big bears and little bears, squirrels and dogs, and the importance of wilderness preservation. In Yellowstone he found a wonderland where animals, largely protected from hunting, could be approached close enough for photography. He came away with the novel insight that animals change their behavior according to how people behave toward them. Eventually, he would learn that wild creatures prosper or decline based on our actions. Within the confines of Yellowstone, as a result of not being hunted,

Top: *Armadillo*, gouache, pen, and ink wash, 1890. Academy for the Love of Learning.

Center: *Red Mouse*, ink, gouache, and pencil, 1884. Academy for the Love of Learning.

Bottom: *Common Skunk*, ink, ca. 1890s. Academy for the Love of Learning.

Above left: Seton's Camp Fire Club of America Medal for Eminent Service, 1906. Philmont Museum.

Above right: "Camp Fire Club Outing, 1913." Seton is right of center, wearing light-colored clothing. Academy for the Love of Learning.

animals had returned to a more natural state—still wary of humans but not terrified. The park was as close as man might come to a return to paradise. Seton would never see hunting in the same light after this visit.

The people he encountered in Yellowstone delighted Seton as well. As in New Mexico, he greatly enjoyed the company of cowboys and old-time Westerners, some of whom he sketched, and many who told tall tales that amused him greatly. He even ran into one cowboy he had known three years earlier in Clayton. Seton related in his autobiography how this man, now relocated to the Yellowstone country under an assumed name, had killed another in self-defense. The naturalist felt a special bond to this cowboy because he may have owed the man his life, or so he wrote in his autobiography. Back in Clayton, a popular and much engaged young woman, "Belle," had invited Seton to attend a dance with her. Seton learned from "the Dude" that one of Belle's many unhappy suitors would be waiting there to ambush whoever accompanied her. Knowing this, Seton opted out. The man who ended up with Belle that evening probably had the same information as Seton, but, unafraid, walked into the ambush with an open mind and ended up killing the attacker. Thus their encounter three years later held special meaning for both the cowboy and Seton: "As soon as I saw those calm gray eyes, I fully recognized him—and he me. My greeting was 'Ha Ha Ha'; his response was a soft 'Ho Ho Ho' and a handshake."

Outside the park, Seton and his wife found time for hunting. Grace was anxious to try out her shooting skills, although she was at the same time conflicted about making the animals suffer. In her two books about their Western travels, Grace gives an account of the animals she killed; at the same time, Seton seems to have done little shooting in his post-Lobo years. At moments of high drama, such as when Grace and a guide stole brass rings from an Indian mummy in Montana, or later, in the Southwest, when she was nearly killed in a mine explosion, her husband was often missing in action. He enjoyed stalking wildlife with a camera or just watching them move about. He also enthusiastically coaxed his wife into shooting game animals, as if he were getting his hunting thrill vicariously through her. After she killed her second elk in 1897, she admitted that she felt "no glory in the achievement." Grace continued hunting through the first nine years of their marriage, until their 1905 encounter with a moose in Ontario that brought their joint hunting adventures to a halt.

There was, however, another wolf hunt, this one along the Little Missouri in North Dakota, where the ranchers had named their favorite wolf nemesis Badlands Billy. As in New Mexico, much of the original hoofed wildlife in North Dakota had been killed off, leaving little for the wolves to dine on except cattle. (This open and wild country had been ranched in earlier years by Theodore Roosevelt, giving him and Seton something in common.) Although the year had passed into mid-September, the multicolored hill country was furiously hot. Grace recalled, "The heat and glare simmered around us like fire. The dogs' tongues nearly trailed in the baked dust, the horses' heads hung low, an iron band seemed ever tightening around my head, as the sun beat down upon all alike with pitiless force." For her the hunt consisted of "heat and rattlesnakes." She dispatched one of the poisonous reptiles with a frying pan. After one dog died from the heat, they gave up the hunt, but "the hunt was not a failure—not for Mountain Billy." Neither was it a failure for Seton, who used the experience for his short story "Badlands Billy, The Wolf That Won."

"John Yancy, Plainsman since 1851," pencil, 1897. Drawn at Yellowstone National Park. Academy for the Love of Learning.

Do you know the three calls of the hunting Wolf:—the long-drawn deep howl, the muster, that tells of game discovered but too strong for the finder to manage alone; and the higher ululation that ringing and swelling is the cry of the pack on a hot scent; and the sharp bark coupled with a short howl that, seeming least of all, is yet a gong of doom, for this is the cry "Close in"—this is the finish?

Illustration from "Badlands Billy" in *Animal Heroes*, pen and ink, ca. 1903. Philmont Museum.

In pristine days the Buffalo herds were followed by bands of Wolves that preyed on the sick, the weak, and the wounded. When the Buffalo were exterminated the Wolves were hard put for support, but the Cattle came and solved the question for them by taking the Buffaloes' place. This caused the wolf-war.

More than three years after the death of Lobo, Seton was once again on the trail of a locally important wolf, but the circumstances were different. This time, the wolf hunter had no lethal intentions. Like Lobo, Billy became one of Seton's literary creations, an animal hero "of unusual gifts and achievements . . . that appeal to the hearts of those who hear them." But unlike Lobo, Billy—through observing the actions of his foster mother—learns how to avoid the traps of man, overcoming all attempts to kill him. In this, Seton set out his basic understanding of animal behavior. Contrary to the popular belief that animals were little more than instinct-driven mechanisms, Seton believed that, along with their instincts, animals also learned how to behave by watching the actions of their parents. More radically, he felt that animals learned by individual experience, gaining the ability to make judgements.

Little more than a year after his encounter with Billy, Seton published *Wild Animals I Have Known*, which reached millions of readers and set off a revolution in the way we perceive nature. Seton gave his readers a new way to think about animals. They were brave, honorable, intelligent, and capable of acting for purposes larger than self-interest; they could take action for the benefit of family members or even their own communities. They were, in effect, much like us. The book ended with an illustration of a nude man flanked by a wolf and a partridge, joined together in the circle of life and surrounded by a spiral of common energy binding us all together.

In 1901, Seton brought out an additional eight wildlife stories in *Lives of the Hunted*, which became another huge seller and built his notoriety still further. At the beginning of the book, he called for what became the wildlife conservation movement.

In my previous books I have tried to emphasize our kinship with the animals by showing that in them we can find the virtues most admired in Man. . . . I have been bitterly denounced, first, for killing Lobo; second, and chiefly, for telling of it, to the distress of many tender hearts. To this I reply: In what frame of mind are my hearers left with regard to the animal? Are their sympathies quickened toward the man who killed him, or toward the noble creature who, superior to every trial, died as he lived, dignified, fearless, and steadfast? . . . My chief motive, my most earnest underlying wish, has been to stop the extermination of harmless wild animals; not for

*their sakes, but for ours, firmly
believing that each of our native
wild creatures is in itself a precious
heritage that we have no right to destroy
or put beyond the reach of our children.
I have tried to stop the stupid and brutal
work of destruction by an appeal—not
to reason: that has failed hitherto—but to
sympathy, and especially the sympathies of
the coming generation.*

*"There is no greater
joy to the truly living
thing than the joy of
being alive, of feeling
alive in every part
and power."*
—*Lives of the
Hunted*

Lives of the Hunted begins with one of Seton's finest stories, "Krag, the Kootenay Ram," in which a magnificent bighorn sheep named Krag finds himself engaged in a lifelong battle against the degenerate hunter Scotty MacDougall, who encounters Krag in the first hour of the animal's life. When Scotty leaves his gun behind so he can capture Krag by hand, he finds himself outmaneuvered by the baby ram and his wise, protective mother. Following their first encounter, Scotty searches for Krag over a fifteen-year period. During that time, Krag grows to become the largest and most powerful bighorn of his generation, renowned for his spectacular horns, the most perfect ever known in that region of Canada. Scotty misses every chance at killing Krag while at the same time becoming obsessed with the idea of possessing the horns. He decides that before he becomes too old he will stalk Krag through the mountains until at last catching the animal, no matter how long it takes. Krag is an animal of great strength and intelligence, but Scotty brings something else to their contest.

> *Scotty, left far behind for a time, trudged steadily, surely, behind him. For added to his tireless strength was the Saxon understreak of brutish grit, of senseless, pig-dogged pertinacity—the inflexible determination that still sticks to its purpose long after sense, reason, and honor have abandoned the attempt, that blinds its owner to his own defeat, and makes him, even when he is downed, still feebly strike—yes, spend his final mite of strength in madly girding at his conqueror, whose quick response, he knows, will be to wipe him out.*

Scotty relentlessly follows Krag in an insane pursuit from autumn into winter, over twelve weeks and five hundred miles. Krag has continually tried to outrun the hunter, to disappear into snowstorms, to hide his tracks among those of other bighorns, but nothing has worked. Scotty knows the mountains and the ways of bighorns, frequently anticipating the course that Krag must take. Krag learns that he must stay five hundred yards ahead of Scotty in order to remain out of gunshot range and finally gets so used to the pursuit that he waits for Scotty to catch up—better under the circumstances to keep the enemy within sight. Bighorn sheep must regularly graze, but Scotty gives Krag so little time that the great animal begins to starve. The rugged journey is no less harsh for Scotty, whose physical deterioration soon matches his mental collapse.

One day the two find themselves on opposing hills, each waiting for the other to make a move. Scotty makes a dummy of himself and sneaks off, leaving Krag to watch his unusually immobile pursuer. The hunter circles around behind. The ambush is anticlimactic—with Krag looking in the wrong direction, Scotty shoots the bighorn from behind, and the hunt is over. Krag's eyes remain open and staring out while Scotty cuts off the head and lugs it back to his shanty. Subsequently, a taxidermist mounts the head, and although selling it would bring a fortune to a poor man like Scotty, he cannot bring himself to part with it. But neither can he bear to look at it. He attaches the head to the cabin wall and then covers it so that he can't see Krag's golden eyes. Scotty is convinced that Krag's spirit lurks in the howling winds outside his cabin, awaiting its chance to get even. Gunder Peak, the place of Krag's birth and death, at last throws an avalanche down on the cabin during an especially violent winter storm. In the spring, visitors find Krag's unharmed head sitting atop Scotty's bones, amid the splinters of what had been his home.

For Seton, Scotty's mania is but one small story within the large-scale self-destructive penchant of Western civilization. Not only does the persecutor lack a valid reason for his destructive action, he lacks any reason at all. Therein lies the madness not just of an individual, but of an entire society oblivious to, if not actively seeking, the destruction of wild nature. Seton's critics could not accept the validity of this premise. Even worse, Krag's sense of morality and ability to reason seemed outrageous to them. Seton refused to back down from his radical assertions. And for that, he paid a price.

Nature Fakers

In early 1903, the revered American nature writer John Burroughs accused Seton and two other nature writers, G. D. Roberts (another Canadian) and William J. Long (an American who spent a great deal of time in Canada), of falsification in their stories. Burroughs's critique appeared in the March issue of *Atlantic Monthly* under the title "Real and Sham Natural History." It was primarily an invective against Long, who Burroughs

Ernest Thompson Seton
ARTIST—LECTURER—AUTHOR

felt had made egregious mistakes—or fabrications—in writing about wild animals. Long and Roberts were outdoorsmen of considerable experience but not naturalists in the same sense as Seton. Burroughs, however, threw Seton in with the other two. He asked, "Are we to believe that Thompson Seton, in his few years of roaming the West, has penetrated farther into the secrets of animal life than all the observers who have gone before him?" The article abandoned any pretense of constructive criticism and bottomed out as personal attack, although Burroughs had met Seton only once and did not yet know about the younger man's extensive nature studies with Native Americans, the basis for Seton's ecological and integrative thinking.

Burroughs was at the time a popular essayist and a national figure who associated with the great men of his time, from Walt Whitman to Theodore Roosevelt. His opinion mattered. The controversy he began played out in the press over the next several years—more as a squabbling among naturalist personalities than as an accounting of the then-known biological facts about wildlife. From today's perspective, one must wonder whether professional jealousy on Burroughs's part may have been involved. The three upstarts were becoming highly popular at a time when the elderly man (sixty-six years old in 1903) may have felt his career was winding down. The entire episode might have been written off as the rant of a cranky old man, except for the response from Long, who counterattacked Burroughs in print, questioning his ability as a naturalist. He took the clever—and, to Seton, embarrassing—tactic of defending both himself and Seton together. Long was an entertaining writer who combined his real knowledge of wildlife with a wild imagination, to the detriment of his stories and, ultimately, to the destruction of his career. Seton didn't like Long's stories any more than

Burroughs did, but he found himself trapped in an association with the other author. He wrote his naturalist friends William Hornaday and Frank Chapman asking advice on handling the situation. The consensus was that Seton should lie low, particularly as he was at the same time launching the Woodcraft movement and couldn't afford bad publicity.

Seton knew he and Burroughs needed to meet in an attempt to settle their differences, or at least to try to understand one another. An opportunity presented itself almost at once when both were invited to an annual literary dinner hosted by Andrew Carnegie. The great capitalist was not the literary sort himself, but an invitation from someone so rich to a lavish party could hardly be ignored, especially when guests such as Mark Twain were expected to show up. Seton decided to confront Burroughs and prove that he too was a legitimate naturalist, although he also sought reconciliation. While still a teenager, he had found in Burroughs the role model he needed while making his own way. Having been the subject of an attack by one of his earliest heroes left Seton hurt; this made their meeting all the more important.

When Burroughs found Seton cordial at the dinner, he decided they could get along. He came to appreciate Seton's abilities as a field naturalist, even if he was not quite convinced about the younger man's ability as a writer. For Seton, the situation was just the reverse; he thought the old transcendentalist a fine writer but a less capable naturalist. By this time, Seton had already traveled through much of North America, while Burroughs had scarcely left home. According to Seton, he made sure the old man recognized this. Even though they parted the evening as friends and Burroughs recanted much of his criticism of Seton in a subsequent *Atlantic Monthly* article, the avalanche of bad publicity set off was already out of control, and it would get worse over the next four years.

By the time he wrote his autobiography, Seton expressed no bitterness toward Burroughs, although his account of their meeting is somewhat suspect, starting with his having placed it in the wrong year, a full twelve months after it took place. He arrived at the party, he wrote later, to find Twain, Burroughs, and novelist William Dean Howells deep in conversation—about him, or so he claimed. Seton launched himself at them,

Top: *A Spotted Disaster* (ocelot), ink wash and gouache, 1897. Academy for the Love of Learning.

Bottom: John Burroughs during a visit to Wyndygoul, ca. 1912. Library and Archives Canada.

Above: John Burroughs Memorial Association Medal, awarded to Seton for *Lives of Game Animals,* 1926. Philmont Museum.

Below: "Seton and taxidermy of Great Blue Heron," ca. 1915. Philmont Museum.

Howells fleeing the scene and Burroughs trying to do so, giving Twain much amusement. Seton pretended to Burroughs to know nothing about the *Atlantic Monthly* article, but persuaded Carnegie to seat the two of them together at table where everyone could be counted on to listen for whatever passed between them. Seton claimed to have skewered the old man with a series of questions, each answered with a short "no." "Mr. Burroughs, did you ever make a special study of wolves? Did you ever hunt wolves? Did you ever live in wolf country?" And so on, before concluding, in effect, with the question, "Then who are you to judge me?" Seton pressed the attack until Burroughs turned red and then "broke down and wept."

For the next several years, Long and Burroughs, along with their respective supporters, continued to snipe at each other through articles and editorial pages of various publications, distracting each other from supporting the important conservation work of men like John Muir, whose lead they should have followed. Seton still made no public statements, although editorial cartoons of the period included him with Long. Finally, Long carried the whole thing too far and earned, for the first time, an attack in print from President Roosevelt in 1907. For a president to get involved in a battle among natural history writers was extraordinary, but Roosevelt could not bear to see any more affronts to his close friend Burroughs. Through his own persistence,

Long had already managed to vanquish most of what little credibility he had left. Not content with relative ruin, he went for complete ruin by attacking Roosevelt in print. Taking on old "Uncle John" was one thing, but trying to bag TR was another—clearly, not a good idea. The outcry against Long convinced him to get out of the nature-writing business, and for Seton the result of Long's self-destructiveness was disastrous.

Roosevelt wrote an article calling Long and his ilk "nature fakers," a term that continues to echo down through the decades. While Roosevelt did not name Seton to that list, he did something else almost as damning—he presented to the

American public a list of legitimate naturalists including Burroughs, Muir, Hornaday, and C. Hart Merriam, among others. Missing from the list: Ernest Thompson Seton. To his dying day, as far as can be told from his writings, Seton continued to admire Roosevelt as much as anyone he ever met. Even after Roosevelt's article was published, Seton remained in occasional friendly contact with him both during and after his presidency, but either he did not realize how much damage had been done to his reputation or he chose to ignore it. Either way, Seton never fully recovered from the nature-faker controversy.

The writer Hamlin Garland, who was a close confidante of many celebrities of his time, intervened with Roosevelt on Seton's behalf and published his conversation after the president's death but during Seton's lifetime. Garland asked TR how he felt about *Wild Animals I Have Known*. Garland quoted the response:

> *As stories based on wild animal life, I have no criticism to make of that book, but Seton in his preface goes too far in emphasizing the scientific value of his tales. If he had brought the book out on its merits as fiction—as a free transcription of animal life, no one would have accused him of "pulling a long bow."*

Garland pointed out Seton's vast documentation of wildlife behavior and, as well, his growing positive influence on youth. Roosevelt, however, remained convinced that a firm line existed between fiction and science. Garland reported his conversation with the president back to Seton. "To be included among 'The Nature Fakers' by Roosevelt and Burroughs was no joke," Garland wrote. This was certainly true, but for the moment there was nothing either of them could do about it.

Seton's career continued to advance, but not getting on TR's list of acceptable naturalists must have hit him much harder than he admitted in print. His interest in writing animal stories began to wane—thereafter, he produced fewer of them. (This could also have been the result of his ongoing promotion of Woodcraft and co-founding the Boy Scouts of America, both of which kept him quite busy.) He felt that he needed to establish his credentials as a naturalist in a way that stories like Lobo and Krag had failed to do. So he became an Arctic explorer, telling the tale in a unique travel book. He wrote one of the first books on animal tracks, and also one of the first books on Indian sign language. And he spent over twenty years compiling a monumental work on North American mammals. In the process, he helped lay the foundations for what would soon emerge as the sciences of ecology and animal behavior.

Two Deaths

Volume one of Seton's great work on North American mammals, *Lives of Game Animals*, begins with a remarkable drawing. *The Thought* shows a nude, beardless Caucasian man, buttocks to the ground, genitalia blanket-covered, right leg back in a kneeling position. He holds with both hands a large sword, and he is ready to strike on downward swing. His left leg is thrust out before him, and on his foot perches a squirrel he is about to kill. (The squirrel represents nature—in its nut planting, it ensures the continuous regeneration of forests.) Behind the figure lies a discarded torch, the abandoned light of truth. Dry bones are scattered by his knee, while above, thin clouds form into wild spirals. We are witnessing his final moment of contemplation, the instant during which he can decide to continue with his purpose or draw back from it. Anything can happen in this place, as thoughts and events are in chaotic motion. Will the sword fall? At what cost?

These questions had personal meaning for Seton. On September 25, 1905, he recorded in his journal a scientific description of a moose killed by his wife during a Canadian canoe trip. (By this time, Seton hunted only with a camera, a new sport he enthusiastically proposed to his lecture audiences.) The death of this moose held special meaning for the couple. Seton described it in *Wild Animals At Home*. Grace wrote about it as well in her second travel book, *Nimrod's Wife*. Their accounts did not precisely match, but given the attention they both gave the incident, it was clearly important to them. Grace wanted to kill her first moose, an endeavor to which Seton gave his full support. When they failed to sight a moose, Seton made a moose caller out of birch bark, imitating the call of a female in estrus. A bull appeared at Seton's call, and Grace, an expert marksman, killed it with two well-placed shots.

The Thought, pen and ink, 1924.

THE. THOUGHT

Writing about it later, Grace claims Seton was not present when the terrible deed took place. Since hunting no longer fit Seton's public persona in 1905, perhaps Grace felt she should remove him from culpability. In his account, Seton makes no attempt to duck his responsibility, admitting to having participated in the event and describing himself unflatteringly as a "Florentine assassin," who afterward killed no more moose and never again used a rifle. Which was not true. There was one exception.

Motivated in part by being rebuked as a nature faker, Seton realized he must change the trajectory of his career to prove himself a professional naturalist, or, in our terms, a biologist. So, in a career that already seemed too full and too busy to add anything more, Seton decided to undertake a journey of exploration to the little-known Northwest Territories in Canada.

He chronicled his 1907 trip in *The Arctic Prairies*, published in 1911. The book was part travelogue, part social commentary, part natural history, and part economic forecasting—a kind of far north version of Thomas Jefferson's *Notes on the State of Virginia*. Accompanied by fellow naturalist Edward A. Preble and Indian guides, the party mapped previously uncharted areas around Aylmer Lake and discovered and named the Earl Grey River. They traveled by canoe, making portages into remote areas beyond Great Slave Lake. Seton drew lovely maps and made a series of small exquisite drawings of everyday scenes along the way. He established new range information for musk ox and caribou, cursed mosquitoes, and explained the ecological relationship between hares and lynx.

Seton recounts his encounter with a lynx on the evening of May 19, 1907, later calling it a "colorless record." His party arrived at a river landing near an Indian village. Men from the village came to watch the visitors make camp, while Seton went on a walk through the forest, taking his camera in case he should find something interesting. He spotted a lynx, and for a reason not explained, returned to the canoe for his rifle. The cat had not moved; Seton killed it on sight, later giving its hide and skull to the American Museum of Natural History. This time, however, he could not justify killing in the name of science. He did not include in *The Arctic Prairies* what he was actually feeling when he killed the lynx, but he did revisit the event in *Lives of Game Animals*:

Seton and Grace still together in 1916. Library and Archives Canada.

> *It sounds all right and clear, but to this day I cannot forget the kitten-like wonder of those big, mild eyes, turned on me as I fired. He fell without a sound, and when I came up, he still gazed without a moan, without a sign of resentment, with nothing but pained surprise, which my conscience translated into: "So this is your love of the wild things."*

Many years later, another killer, Aldo Leopold, reported a similar experience. Like Seton, as a young man Leopold gave little thought to the meaning of his deadly actions. In his book *A Sand County Almanac*, he shares a similar moment of awakening consciousness after he and some companions blast away at a mother wolf and her cubs.

> *We reached the old wolf in time to watch a fierce green fire dying in her eyes. I realized then, and have known ever since, that there was something new to me in those eyes —something*

known only to her and the mountain. I was young then, and full of trigger-itch; I thought that because fewer wolves meant more deer, that no wolves would mean hunters' paradise. But seeing the green fire die, I sensed that neither the wolf nor the mountain agreed with such a view.

Seton had at last fully internalized the meaning of Lobo's death. After his return from the Arctic, he dedicated himself almost fully to the cause of wildlife conservation, both in his writing and in his work with Scouting and Woodcraft. With *The Thought*, Seton shows that the Sword of Damocles still hangs precariously above us, waiting for us to decide what to do next. The eyes of nature look upon us, and wonder.

A Call against Arms

Seton believed that he had gathered enough data and made enough drawings to create a major work on the mammals of Manitoba. Fortunately, with encouragement from Roosevelt and from William Hornaday, a prominent biologist, he instead took on a larger project, publishing in 1909 the two-volume *Lives of Northern Animals*. There had never been anything like it. Introducing novelties such as animal range maps, Seton compiled all the available information he could find about a variety of mammalian species of the northern United States into Canada. Hornaday wrote a highly favorable review in *The Nation*, and then, privately to Seton: "Truly, it is a grand Work; but is no better than I expected. . . . In writing the review I had to restrain myself from praising the book so much that I would defeat my own purpose." Hornaday even offered Seton the presidency of the Bison Society, one of the earliest conservation organizations—a great honor—but Seton had to turn it down due to other commitments. A year later, he received what may have been the most cherished letter of his life, from President Roosevelt:

Top: *The Leap for Life.* Illustration for *The Arctic Prairies*, ink wash and gouache, 1910. Philmont Museum.

Bottom: *Musk Ox*, ink wash, 1907. Philmont Museum.

I have read through your two volumes, and I can hardly speak too highly of them. I regard your work as one of the most valuable contributions any naturalist has made to the life histories of American mammals. In fact I do not know anything that quite parallels your work. The book you have written is one of those books which combine great present interest with permanent value. I think that the lover of outdoors will want it in his library a century hence, just as we who care for outdoors nowadays feel that it must be in our libraries at the present time.

Seton was thrilled by the reception of his work; it gave him the recognition he had long sought. His reputation as a leading naturalist now set, he decided to create an even grander work, which would take him twenty years to complete.

In the meantime, while he slowed the pace of his writing, Seton continued his work as one of the primary activists for wildlife conservation. In 1913, he took an essential role in promoting the first significant piece of American conservation legislation. Environmental historians have taken note of the 1916 convention for the protection of migratory birds, signed by the United States and Great Britain, and the 1918 legislation that implemented it. Less discussed, however, is the Migratory Bird Act, also known as the Weeks-McLean Act, from five years earlier. The act was stunning in its implications, greatly expanding the role of the federal government. Although Seton was not yet a U.S. citizen, his reputation trumped that problem, and he received a letter from Glen Buck, an associate of Henry Ford, asking for help.

National Academy of Sciences Daniel Giraud Elliot Medal for Preeminence in Zoology, 1928, for *Lives of Game Animals.*

Mr. Henry Ford of the Ford Motor Company of Detroit and myself are deeply interested in the legislation now pending before congress which has for its purpose the preservation of bird life.

    I believe that the Weeks bill, which forbids the slaughter of all migratory birds and places their protection under the United States Department of Agriculture—which in effect takes over the ownership of all migratory birds by the Federal Government—is a sound measure in all respects and should become a law. It has already passed the house and there is no reason why it should not pass the senate. As far as I have been able to determine the only reason why this bill has not become a law is that there has been no enthusiastic and well-directed energy back of it.

The Weeks-McLean Act set a precedent of the highest importance: the federal government would hereafter have the authority to intervene on behalf of wildlife. From anti-pollution laws to general preservation of plants and animals to endangered species legislation, every subsequent piece of environmental legislation has built upon this humble beginning. (Indeed, Seton considered the legislation "essential" to the future of wildlife conservation in America.) In trying to get the legislation passed, Buck also lined up John Burroughs to help. And so the three men—representing Henry Ford as well as themselves—traveled to Washington in January 1913 to lobby two senators who were holding up the bill. Seton recalled that he did most of the talking; the elderly Burroughs mostly contributed his presence. Thus did America's two greatest living naturalists help create a milestone in the history of America's environmental movement.

In 1920, Seton returned to the work of creating what became the nonfiction masterwork of his career, *Lives of Game Animals*: "An Account of those Land Animals

Plate XL. — Details of Hoary Marmot.

in America north of the Mexican Border, which are considered 'Game,' either because they have held the Attention of Sportsmen, or received the Protection of Law." Sprawling over 3,115 pages in four volumes, the work included 1,500 art illustrations by the author, fifty range maps covering over a hundred species, and numerous wildlife photographs. Doubleday, Doran & Company published the massive set between 1925 and 1928. Seton had promised delivery to the publisher in 1923, but the naturalist instead took another eight years of full-time work to complete the project; during that time, his output of other writing practically came to a halt. He stopped lecturing. He stopped making money. He disappeared from public view after more than two decades as a celebrity.

Although *Lives of Game Animals* met with literary success, it was too large to reach a mass audience. Seton never again regained the level of attention he had enjoyed at the beginning of the 1920s. But he expressed no regrets. Not everyone has the luxury of completing a life's work in such a spectacular fashion. He shared his thoughts with his longtime friend and colleague, ornithologist Frank Chapman:

I had some sorrows, but great joy, in finishing this work. My bookkeeper could easily show a heavy deficit, especially in the cancellation of lectures and refusals of commissions in order that nothing might prevent my finishing. Yet I know that I did the right thing. And I am weak enough even now to find pleasure in turning over and reading some of the chapters which are so very much a part of myself.

Practically all the illustrations are from my own hand. A few that were contributed by others are plainly marked. The dates of some of my illustrations, back as far as 1880, show how long I had been in accumulating the material. At that time, of course, I did not have the plan in mind; but from 1897 when I conceived it, I have lost no opportunity of making drawings or gathering facts, with a view to this very publication.

Top: *The Heliograph,* pen and ink, ca. 1920s. Academy for the Love of Learning.

Bottom: *Details of the Hoary Marmot,* pen and ink, ca. 1920s. Philmont Museum.

With the publication of *Lives of Game Animals*, Seton became a poet for conservation. The work is a wondrous encyclopedia of wildlife, filled with measurements and descriptions, stories and histories, observations and speculations, slaughter and preservation. Its "synoptic" drawings are unique among biology books, showing the animal for its character. The section on the gray wolf begins with an illustration titled *Undismayed,* in which a standing wolf, canines prominent, stands at the center with a crown over his head—Lobo Rex—all fierce and ready to fight. Dogs, traps, arrows, poison, and cannons assail the wolf. In the background, two people hiding behind a wagon draw a bead on the wolf with rifles. Still farther back is a building that might be a factory—civilization. Put in, almost at random, are three mysterious circles, each with a flying cross or double-S shape within. The symbols are known as *ollins* (named after the Aztec word for movement), a nearly universal symbol found across space and historical time from Celtic Ireland to Southeast Asia to the Navajo lands of the American Southwest. For Seton, the ollins represented the essential aspects of nature: change, motion, and interrelationship.

Seton accomplished something remarkable and daring in these drawings. His animals often wear expressions of joy or triumph; the drawings are not infrequently humorous in tone. They are a representation—based on Seton's decades of experience—of animals overcoming seemingly impossible odds in order to live. The drawings are inherently ecological; that is, they express the notion of an animal living as a part of its environment, a connection that is at once both physical and spiritual.

By contrast, the text is frequently blood soaked with tragic and sometimes chilling stories of the wanton destruction of wildlife. Often these are accounts of individual actions, sometimes jarringly abrupt, such as the hunter who takes pleasure in the beauty of a jaguar looking "right in his eye and gently waving his tail . . . so he killed it." Other accounts are of collective destruction. In the eighteenth and nineteenth centuries, Seton records, scores of men and boys would form armies to wage war on animal life, killing hundreds of creatures for no evident purpose.

Top: *Undismayed* (wolf). Illustration for *Lives of Game Animals*, pen and ink, 1920s. Philmont Museum.

Bottom: *The Alderman and the Apple* (aka *The Ambush for the Prairie Dog*). From *Lives of the Hunted*, gouache, ca. 1900. Academy for the Love of Learning.

Did human hand ever set on paper a more loathsome story of insensate destruction? These vile butchers did not need the meat, or the hides, for they destroyed them. They did not seek the real joys of the chase, for the joys were over before the massacre began. There is no such joy in a shambles.

They did not need the land, for it was one mountainous primeval forest. No one pretended that the wild things were a serious menace. . . . There is absolutely no shadow of excuse.

Amid the sad stories of carnage, *Lives of Game Animals* contains a wealth of remarkable facts. For instance, marmots—high-mountain woodchucks that look like giant dark prairie dogs—purr like cats. Pocket gophers turn the soil in dry and high-mountain environments, taking the place of earthworms, which do not live in such areas. Porcupines can have as many as 36,450 quills, with each quill supporting one thousand barbs, totaling more than thirty-six million barbs protecting the animal. Grizzly bears and mountain lions generally give way to porcupines and skunks when they meet in the woods. Because he was among the first to recognize the relational complexity of nature, Seton made his nonfiction books on nature mirror that complexity: somewhat messy in organization, red in tooth and claw, endless in its detail—like life itself.

The third volume of *Lives of Game Animals* ends with a lament for the disappearing wild, a short poetic essay in which Seton decries what has been lost and expresses his anguish and dread of an apocalyptic future. Published in 1927, the essay includes these words:

And farther yet my soul-view reaches in the years. I see the only logical completeness of this hell-born mania to Destroy—This—surely this: the nation possessed of it, will certainly destroy itself."

DESERT DRINK.   E.T.SETON.

The Myth.   E.T.SETON

Right: *The Last of the Race,* pen and ink, ca. 1920s. Academy for the Love of Learning.

Below: *Antelope Head,* oil on panel, n.d. Philmont Museum.

THE LAST OF THE RACE   E.T. SETON.

CHAPTER FOUR

Woodcraft and the World

The beginning of the outdoor education movement is a drama about three men. Their great ambitions, drive for personal celebrity, and need to be recognized led to the turbulent beginnings of the Boy Scouts in England and America. Worldwide, tens of millions of boys have taken part in Scouting, making its programs in outdoor education and citizenship one of the great cultural developments of the twentieth century. Scouting could not have developed as it did without all three of these men.

Ernest Thompson Seton felt that he should have been recognized as the principal founder of the worldwide Scouting movement. Dan Beard, another early promoter of outdoor boy culture, also claimed this distinction. Robert S. S. Baden-Powell was less direct in his claim of primary authorship but accepted the credit offered by others to him as the true originator. Scouters and historians continue to debate the question of who founded the movement.

Beard, who like Seton was an artist and writer, had published books for boys extolling the virtue of outdoor life and activities from the 1880s. In 1905, he created the framework for a boys' camping organization and used the term "Scouts." Baden-Powell, one of the most famous men of his time in the English-speaking world—he held the titles of Lord and General—was a hero of the Second Boer War in South Africa. He had overseen the creation of a paramilitary organization for noncombatant boys to supplement regular troops in that conflict. He wrote about the military aspects of scouting and, after he returned to England, began to think about creating a patriotic organization for boys that would prepare them for future military service. "B-P," as he is often called, published *Scouting for Boys* in 1908; within months, the Boy Scouts in England enrolled over a hundred thousand members. The movement soon spread to Canada and Europe and then, in 1910, came to America.

Seton's contribution to this movement came about through a set of principles he summarized with the term "Woodcraft." He began his organization earlier than the others, on his property in Connecticut. By May 1900, due to the phenomenal success of *Wild Animals I Have Known*, *The Biography of a Grizzly*, and *The Trail of the Sandhill Stag*, Seton felt confident about purchasing "the dream of my life," a woodland tract in Cos Cob, part of Greenwich, Connecticut, far enough from his Manhattan apartment

Left: Seton in his role as "Black Wolf," ca. 1915. Library and Archives Canada.

Below: Seton on bench, ca.1910. Library of Congress.

Seton's home of Wyndygoul. Historical Society of the Town of Greenwich.

(about thirty-five miles) to be a real retreat, yet close enough to keep up with business and social affairs. Seton first built a rustic cabin, and then a mansion of his own design. The estate consisted of

a hundred acres of woodland, which they have named Wyndygoul, for one of the [Seton] estates in Scotland. The house stands on the highest point of the tract. It is Spanish in effect, the lower story of rough-hewn green-tipped rocks, quarried on the place; the upper story of creamy pink stucco. The low red roof, wide verandas, low entrance door and quaint arrangement of windows are interesting and picturesque. The Englishman's love of solidity is shown in the thick walls, massive cornices of natural wood, and in the heavy beams in the studio ceiling.

Finding the time to design and oversee construction of the house must have been difficult for Seton. Only a couple of weeks after the purchase, he and Grace were on their way to Europe for the summer, including a special trip to Norway to study reindeer. He was working on a new book as well. In June, he compiled a list of useful plants and notes relating to camping and other outdoor skills under a brief notation, "2 Little Savages," the conceptual beginning of the Woodcraft movement. He managed to spend time in New York during the early fall before going on a lecture tour in October and November.

The following year, Seton introduced squirrels, deer, and other animals to his property in order to create his own private park, protected by a fence to keep out dogs as well as human trespassers. It did not turn out to be as private as he had wished. Seton had inadvertently fenced out a group of young boys for whom his woodlands had long served as a recreation area. The naturalist's regular absences made protecting the place difficult—the boys showed their displeasure by vandalizing the property, tearing down the fence, and painting "wicked pictures" on the entry gate. In the spring of 1902, Seton confronted the boys outside the gate about the ongoing attacks, but they merely laughed at him. A neighbor advised him to bring charges against the delinquents, but Seton refused to call in the law and decided instead to find another way to handle the issue. "I knew something of boys," he wrote, "in fact, I am much of a boy myself."

Seton had long thought about organizing an outdoor activity scheme for boys; in March 1902, he found the opportunity to do so. The school term had not yet ended, so just before Easter he visited the local school and asked permission to address all the boys twelve years old and older. He invited them to join him for a weekend of camping in teepees, canoeing on a newly built lake, and running about his property as much as they pleased. He asked them to arrive Friday afternoon after school. The twelve boys present gave back to him nothing more than the sullen silence typical of that age group. Always an optimist, Seton returned home and put together provisions for twenty boys in case a few more showed up. He hired a man to serve as cook and general helper. On Friday, an hour past the time when the boys had been invited, Seton felt anxious about his experiment prematurely ending.

The moment of deepest silence was broken by a horde of forty-two boys arriving simultaneously. They entered what Seton called a "council ring," a feature that soon thereafter, in large part because of Seton's promotion of the idea, made its appearance at just about every summer camp in America. It was not clear what would happen once the boys arrived, but soon Seton had them swimming in the lake and swarming over his property to burn off energy. They spent the next hour engaging in a wild, chaotic frenzy of activity, largely unsupervised in a more innocent age before the advent of liability suits. Fortunately, no one was seriously injured, although the horde worked up an appetite that cleaned out a weekend's worth of food in just one meal. Afterward, Seton spun spellbinding tales of the far West and Indians and adventure. His most daring move, however, was to help the boys organize to elect their own leaders, reserving for himself the position of "Medicine Man," an advisory role. Suddenly faced with taking personal responsibility, the boys rose to the challenge and brought order to their

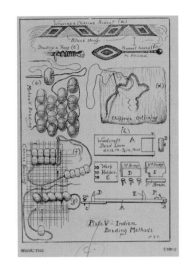

The Sinawa Tribe at the Village of Standing Rock (Wyndygoul), ca. 1904. Philmont Museum.

Top: *Guy Gave a Leap of Terror and Fell*, illustration from *Two Little Savages*, ink and gouache, 1903. Philmont Museum.

Bottom: *If You Kill Any Songbirds, I'll Use the Rawhide on Ye*, illustration from *Two Little Savages*, ink, pencil, and gouache, 1903. Academy for the Love of Learning.

ranks largely on their own. At the end of the weekend, Seton felt his camping experiment was a success.

By coincidence, a series of articles on outdoor activities for boys that Seton had sold to the *Ladies' Home Journal* began to appear the following month. The installments of "Ernest Thompson Seton's Boys" were published in the *Journal* every month from May to November. His innovative concept for camping, games, and nature study took off among boys almost at once. He finally found time to make a journal entry about the new concept on July 1, 1902, writing, "Went to Summit, N. J. to visit the Seton Indians. [Took?] a teepee also bows and arrows—had a wonderful time." He added to the entry an additional note at a later time, "This is the first organized band. This is the foundation of the Woodcraft Indians." Inspired by news of the idea, new boys' tribes sprang up in the region, informally organized by other adult leaders following the Seton model. The participants at first called themselves "Seton Indians" after their charismatic founder. By the end of summer 1902, about two thousand boys had participated in "the study of woodcraft" during camping excursions.

Seton could not have anticipated this level of success so soon after launching the new program, but its timing could not have been more fortuitous, as he was ready to publish his most ambitious literary work to date. *Two Little Savages: The Story of Two Boys Who Lived as Indians Do* began its appearance in serialized form in January 1903 and in book form by the end of the year. This partly autobiographical account of his life appeared, like the earlier articles, in the *Ladies' Home Journal*.

And, like *Studies in the Art Anatomy of Animals* and *Wild Animals I Have Known*, it has remained in print through all the subsequent decades. Part coming-of-age story and part how-to, *Two Little Savages* provided inspiration to boys who loved the outdoors and offered a model for progressive education—all in the guise of a simple story about a couple of backwoods boys, their friends, and their adventures in the wild. Seton felt that stimulating the imagination, teaching personal responsibility and self-reliance, proselytizing respect for nature, and presenting the value systems of traditional Native America would form children into socially responsible and productive adults.

By February 1903, Seton had begun a popular lecture series about Indians and wildlife that occupied him through several decades. Lecture tickets at that time cost from fifty cents to one dollar; Seton regularly sold out lecture halls, dividing the proceeds

with speaker-tour impresario J. B. Pond. During the second summer, the number of Seton Indians more than doubled from the first. The *New York Herald* gave the white Indians an enthusiastic response:

> *An Indian uprising of unprecedented proportions is reported throughout the country among the Seton tribes. During the summer more than fifty tribes have been heard from. You may search in vain in American history for any mention of the Indians. Their braves, several thousand strong, are merely so many bright, adventurous American boys who are playing at being Indians, but with tribes so carefully organized and with customs and games to play so artfully chosen that any real Indians might well feel at home among them. The founder of these tribes,*

Clockwise from top left: Wyndygoul—council and war dance, ca. 1905. Library of Congress.
A teepee at Camp Flying Eagles, Wyndygoul, ca. 1905. Library of Congress.
Deer hunt (tracking and hunting game), Wyndygoul, ca. 1905. Library of Congress.
Salmon matching (a water sports game), ca. 1905. Library of Congress.

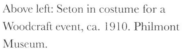

Above left: Seton in costume for a Woodcraft event, ca. 1910. Philmont Museum.

Above right: Wyndygoul camp rock, ca. 1904. Library and Archives Canada.

Middle: Shirt worn by Seton, incorporating antique pieces with his own Woodcraft designs. Philmont Museum. Photo credit: Dave Emery.

Bottom: Leggings worn by Seton, Comanche, ca. 1880. Philmont Museum. Photo credit: Dave Emery.

and in short the big chief of them all, is Mr. Thompson-Seton, the naturalist, whose name they have taken. They are the first of the Setons.

It is not clear what "real Indians" might have felt had they witnessed this spectacle of white boys playing Indian, but "at home among them" probably would not be on the list. So as not to offend a society where white racism was the norm, Seton wrote reassuringly to parents that in choosing the culture of native peoples as his model for children's activities, "Our watchword then is: 'The best things of the best Indians.'"

The Seton Indians were a decentralized, anti-authoritarian group that practiced egalitarian socialism, personal self-sufficiency, woodsy survivalism, and a deep respect for and integration with the rhythms of nature. Mindful of these characteristics, academics have suggested that the group was an attack on modernity itself. However high the Seton Indians may be on today's political incorrectness scale, at the time there was nothing else like it. In a rapidly industrializing society, the Seton Indians provided a way to connect young people to nature, the outdoors, and even the customs of another race. Seton kept busy answering letters from his Indians as well as running his own camp on his Cos Cob estate. Boys could enter his home camp by just showing up at the gate and asking to be let in. And Seton, who turned forty-three that summer, loved playing Indian himself. He dressed in Indian costumes—primarily homemade, the Woodcraft way—to lead the boys in Indian dances. He always dressed to suit the weather, sometimes appearing nearly nude (in Indian fashion). The boys wore horsehair scalps tied to the belts of their swimming trunks. City visitors must have shaken their heads in disbelief. Manhattan was little more than forty-five minutes and a couple of centuries away.

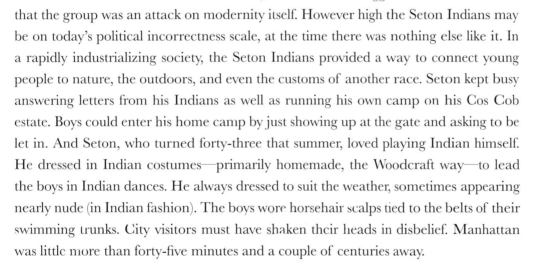

Its wood, almost as wild as a forest in appearance; its lake with rocky shores and a series of cliffs breaking directly down to the water's edge, have been left untouched or else improved with an art which leaves them all perfectly natural. Flocks of wild ducks fly about the lake while pheasants and other birds fill the wood . . . There are half a dozen teepees surrounding a painted rock which bears the emblem of the tribe. The teepees are originals collected by Mr. Seton. One of them is still decorated with human scalps, and all are decorated with elaborate designs in color, the work of Indian artists.

With a totem pole and painted rocks in the camp, the boys, aged around twelve to sixteen, learned cooking, firemaking, tree identification, swimming, and archery (shooting at deer targets made from burlap and stuffed with straw), and engaged in canoe races on water and over land portages. The summer camps continued at Wyndygoul until 1912, when Seton sold the estate and soon moved to a new property only six miles away named DeWinton (in honor of his early Canadian home outside Carberry), and a somewhat quieter life there. He built another large house on this property, which was also in Greenwich (though not in Cos Cob). In 1903, Seton's enthusiasm for the project could not have been higher. In addition to the book version of *Two Little Savages*, he printed the first pamphlet of what would become an ever-growing series of annually updated field guides to outdoor living that came to be called the Birch Bark Roll. The first version, titled *How to Play Indian* (based on the articles "Ernest Thompson Seton's Boys"), was in reprintings named the *Red Book* because of the color of its cover. Its purpose was to give "Directions for organizing a tribe of boy Indians and making their teepees in true Indian style."

Most boys love to play Indian and would like to learn more about doing it. They want to know about all the interesting things the Indians did that are possible for them to do. It adds great pleasure to the lives of such boys when they knew that they can go right out in the holidays and camp in the woods just as the Indians did, and make all their own weapons in Indian style as well as rule themselves after the manner of a band of Redmen.

As the totem for the nation of the Seton Indians (also known as Woodcraft Indians), Seton and his boys decided upon a "White or Silver Buffalo," an insignia later adopted by the Boy Scouts as its highest award for service to Scouting. The Woodcraft movement, however, differed significantly from the later organization because of its emphasis on Native American culture as a model for activities and values. Because of the enthusiastic response and unpredictably fast growth in membership in the beginning, Seton's pamphlet guided the many boys who wanted to take part in his scheme in their own communities. The thirty-two pages of the *Red Book* covered basic organizing principles, including laws (some of which were adopted by the Boy Scouts) and the designation of chiefs (officers). The laws included prohibitions against setting wildfires, harming songbirds, and breaking game laws. Chiefs—the boys themselves—took a variety of leadership roles, from organizing day and evening activities, to judging contests and awarding "scalps" and feathers, to wearing badges identifying their tribes and talents.

Both badges and scalps were available through Abercrombie & Fitch; horsehair scalps cost ten cents each or twelve for a dollar. The bulk of the booklet was a section on teepee construction, decoration, and traditional use. The instructions may have been somewhat challenging for anyone not already familiar with this kind of shelter—nearly all of Seton's readers—so teepees also could be purchased from Abercrombie & Fitch.

Seton's egalitarian approach, based on his understanding of traditional American Indian political organization, was in stark contrast to the adult command structure that Baden-Powell would develop for Scouting a few years later. Seton introduced a second innovation that he would call "honors by standards." He did not accept competition as the sole force guiding relations in the biological world of wildlife or in our social world. He was one of the first naturalists to note that cooperation is also an important survival strategy for many animal species. Like other educators of the Progressive Era around the turn of the twentieth century, he felt that cooperation was a better model for society than competition. The kind of competition that Seton particularly disliked is now called a zero-sum game, where one person can benefit only at the expense of another.

This he contrasted to the more appropriate goal of personal achievement, a high value in traditional tribal life. Seton's boys competed against a general standard rather than against one another. As a symbol of accomplishment, feathers were awarded for ability in swimming, firemaking, plant identification, and so forth.

In addition to the resident Cos Cob boys, who named themselves the "Sinawa" tribe after an actual native group that had once lived there, other newly formed bands came to Wyndygoul for personal instruction from "Black Wolf," the Indian name Seton took for himself around this time. On weekends when

Facing, top: Woodcraft cabin at DeWinton, ca. 1917. Philmont Museum.

Facing, middle: Woodcraft meeting, ca. 1920. Library and Archives Canada.

Facing, bottom: Seton in DeWinton woods, ca. 1917. Philmont Museum.

Below: Seton with three Blackfeet Indians, ca. 1917. Library of Congress.

Seton with early group of Woodcraft Indians, ca. 1904. Library and Archives Canada.

there were no visiting tribes on his estate, Black Wolf traveled to work with boys at their home camps elsewhere in New York, Connecticut, and perhaps other states. An article of that time in the *Greenwich News* included a list of Woodcraft Indian boys, two of whom, George White and Leonard Clark, were later interviewed about their experiences, in the 1970s. White, who would have been around eleven years old in 1902, may have attended the very first camp. He continued his participation at least through 1906. He confirmed "the main points of Seton's story" about the origins of the Woodcraft Indians. The Woodcraft boys remained tied to the personality of Black Wolf, whose greatest appeal was to tribes in the region with which he could keep in personal contact. With each subsequent printing of the Birch Bark Roll, Seton's influence on other summer camping programs grew. There were probably never more than a few thousand Woodcraft Indians, but many—maybe most—summer camp programs throughout the country adopted aspects of Seton's youth program in the decades after he first introduced it. Seton had neither the inclination nor the patience for institution-building, so Woodcraft remained primarily a conceptual set of principles. But the popularity of his ideas proved the need—and the demand—for youth outdoor education programs. Seton promoted Woodcraft not just in the United States, but also in England, where he lectured on the "Red Indian" and passed out copies of the Birch Bark Roll. By its fourth summer the Woodcraft Indians had garnered a great deal of attention, but also, to Seton's lasting fury, an imitator.

The Challenge

Historians have concentrated on Seton's complex relationship with Robert Baden-Powell, which over time moved through stages of admiration, rivalry, intense dislike, acceptance, and long-standing grudge-holding. Both men could perhaps be accused of exhibiting monomania, now an antique word, but one known in the nineteenth century when it was used by Herman Melville in describing Captain Ahab, the whale-obsessed captain of the doomed ship in *Moby-Dick*. Both Seton and Baden-Powell were similarly obsessed with their respective plans for youth education. Less well-understood is that Seton's anger about what he regarded as the theft of his ideas did not begin with

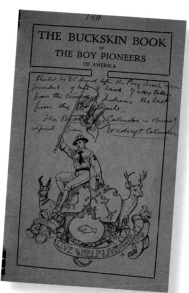

Baden-Powell, but rather with Dan Carter Beard, a longtime acquaintance and also an early conservationist. Beard, like Seton and Baden-Powell, also had his own agenda.

Seton and Beard had very different upbringings, but they also had much in common—which may be why they became antagonistic rivals. Both were illustrators of note; Beard was the better known of the two before 1898. Both were associated with zoological and ornithological societies as well as the Camp Fire Club of America and the American Museum of Natural History. Both shared an interest in forestry. Years after the termination of their friendship, Beard wrote about woodcraft and wolves. Both were popular with boys, writing well-received columns for *Boys' Life*, among other publications. Beard was the author of the 1882 *What to Do and How to Do It: The American Boy's Handy Book*. An advocate for the outdoor life and nature study, he already had a reputation among boys long before Seton began his program for boys.

But there was an important difference between Seton and Beard. Seton started the *first* organization designed exclusively for outdoor education, the one on which all subsequent organizations would be modeled, no matter how different in detail. Dan Beard founded the second. In April 1905, when Beard became editor of *Recreation*, a wildlife magazine for which Seton had written, he announced the formation of a new youth group, The Sons of Daniel Boone, named for the famous frontiersman because of his early advocacy of game laws. Seton felt betrayed by a man he had considered a friend. Beard, however, could point to his publication record of articles and books for boys—one far longer than Seton's. In May, Beard published an invitation to the boys of England and America: "Whether we owe allegiance to the brave old British lion or the

Above left: Dan Beard at Boy Scouts of America camp, Blue Ridge, North Carolina, 1922. Academy for the Love of Learning.

Above right: Seton's annotated copy of Dan Beard's *The Buckskin Book of the Boy Pioneers of America*, 1911. Academy for the Love of Learning

fierce American eagle makes little difference, we are all boys together and are going to unite in one brotherhood for the preservation of our brothers in fur, scales, feathers, and bark."

Unlike the organic beginnings of the Woodcraft Indians, the Sons of Daniel Boone began as an announcement in a magazine. Instead of tribes, the Sons were to organize as "forts," and instead of Indian symbols, each fort would have, as a kind of fetish, an old gun representing the white pioneers of yore.

In olden times, our pioneer ancestors were wont to keep a record, by notches on the stock of their rifles, of the deer or bear killed; and even in times of savage warfare of the number of Indian scalps taken. But in these days we do not propose to hunt the poor, persecuted Indians or scalp them as our half savage ancestors did, and while we want to emulate these ancestors in all their sturdy, manly qualities we will only use our tally gun for a record of good deeds we do in the preservation of game and forests.

While real Indians may have been glad to learn of the Sons' benign intentions, Seton was not pleased. Not only did Woodcraft now have a rival, it honored the white frontiersman as an alternate model to the virtues of the Native American. Seton must have realized that there was room in the woods for additional boys' groups, but this one lifted a lot of his ideas without credit. In any event, while Seton's Woodcrafters continued with their modest success, Beard's group fizzled. He left *Recreation* for a job at the *Woman's Home Companion*, taking the Sons with him, and renaming them the Boy Pioneers of America. The group did no better under a different name and later was absorbed into the Boy Scouts. The one thing Beard's organization did accomplish was to create a rift between him and Seton, which would erupt into verbal warfare a few years later.

More significant as a challenge to Woodcraft was the scheme of Robert Baden-Powell, who formed a youth group of his own in Great Britain. Seton remained a British citizen until 1930, and like most of his countrymen, he had taken a sharp interest in the war against the Boers in South Africa, an area then divided into four mini-states. The war came about as ethnic Dutch residents found themselves at a disadvantage amid an influx of British colonists. Control of gold fields was at stake. For over two years, beginning in the latter part of 1899 and bloodily continuing into the spring of 1902, the Boer light cavalry put up a spirited fight, but was inevitably overcome by the irresistible might of the British war machine. Thousands of people died, including large numbers of black Africans who got in the way of white imperialism. By the time the war ended, the British public had grown tired of the whole mess, but it paid rapt attention at the beginning, especially over the siege of Mafeking, a British stronghold threatened with certain defeat by the Boers. In command of the defense was Colonel Robert Baden-Powell, whose exploits over the seven months of the siege got the English caught up in the drama of the war. Nothing succeeds like exceeding expectations. Baden-Powell was expected by military leaders on both sides to fail in his effort to hold the town. Instead, he weathered the assault and became known ever after as the Hero of Mafeking. Under his authority, boys as young as twelve were recruited as messengers and lookouts; that is, as scouts. After the war, Baden-Powell wrote a military book on scouting that was taken up by boys still excited by his war reputation. He next wrote a civilian version designed as a guide for youth to outdoor activities and to citizenship. *Scouting for Boys*, released in 1908, launched the international Boy Scout movement. Thus, single-handedly, Baden-Powell founded the most successful youth organization of the century. Or so the story goes.

A comparison of *Scouting for Boys* and the Birch Bark Roll (1906 edition) shows striking similarities between the two works: a significant finding, since Seton's book predates that of Baden-Powell. While Baden-Powell acknowledged that certain games for boys included in his work owed their origin to Seton, he did not admit that many of the organizing principles of Scouting also came from Seton. Revisionist historians have accused Baden-Powell of just about everything imaginable, but for Seton, Baden-Powell was, like Burroughs, a personal hero. Just a few years earlier, Seton had been deeply hurt by Burroughs, but the fellow naturalists found a path to reconciliation. The situation with Baden-Powell was different; the wound was much deeper, more agonizing, and ultimately without cure. Seton, who continued to admire the English hero for his military record, eventually accused the famous general of not giving him credit for the contributions of his Woodcraft principles to Scouting.

Seton's interest in meeting the Hero of Mafeking began in 1905, a year or so after Seton delivered his first lectures on Woodcraft in England. A mutual acquaintance arranged an introduction for the two men, resulting in Seton inviting the general to one of his lectures scheduled to take place in the

Baden-Powell overshadows Seton in a commemorative stamp from Antigua and Barbuda, 2002. Academy for the Love of Learning.

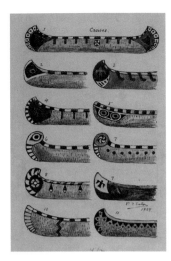

spring of 1906—a meeting that did not take place until October. (It began a fascinating correspondence between the two men; see Appendix 3.) That summer, Seton sent a copy of the most recent version of the Birch Bark Roll to the general. Baden-Powell responded at once:

1 Aug. 06
Dear Sir

I am sincerely grateful for your kindness in forwarding me your interesting Birch Bark.
It may interest you to know that I had been drawing up a scheme with a handbook to it for the education of boys as scouts—which essentially runs much on the lines of yours. So I need hardly say your work has a very special interest to me.
I should very much like to meet you if you are at any time in England—and in any case if you would allow me to send you a copy of my scheme later on (it is not yet printed completely), and give me your criticism of it I should be very grateful indeed.
Believe me—with many thanks,

Yours truly,
R. S. S. Baden Powell

Seton did believe Baden-Powell—for a while. In October, he received a letter from the general that included a comment of particular importance: "If we can work together in the same direction I sh' be very glad indeed—for I am sure there are great possibilities before us." From Seton's perspective, this letter and the next several that followed marked Baden-Powell's acknowledgement that the two of them had entered into a relationship; they would collaborate in creating an important youth movement. The general's perspective is more difficult to understand. Did he really mean to suggest a partnership? Did he purposefully mislead Seton, lulling the naturalist into giving up his cherished ideas for the use of the English organization? Or did Baden-Powell not realize the possible consequences of being flip? By design or by accident, this letter set the two on a collision course.

Another question arises here, equally mystifying. From the beginning, Baden-Powell's "scheme"—his word—had an underlying militarist theme. The civilian *Scouting for Boys* drew significantly from his earlier military manual, *Aids to Scouting*. With an emphasis on patriotism and duty to country, religious (meaning Christian) observation, adult command structure, and adoption of military-style uniforms and badges, *Scouting for Boys* made no secret of a primary goal—preparing boys for possible military service. Seton's Woodcraft was primarily about recreation and nature study. Before World War I, Woodcraft placed no emphasis on patriotic service to the state, and instead emphasized social responsibility to the local community. Although Seton clearly admired Jesus and his teachings, Christianity did not enter into Woodcraft. The movement instead offered a nature-based, non-dogmatic, secular spirituality. The Woodcraft Indians barely wore clothes, let alone uniforms. To be sure, the values of Scouting and Woodcraft were by no means mutually exclusive, and the Boy Scouts adopted—or adapted—many Woodcraft concepts into its program. Nonetheless, it was obvious from the start that Seton and Baden-Powell had fundamental differences in their worldview. The general got many good ideas from Woodcraft for use by the Scouts. It is not at all clear that Scouting gave anything whatsoever back to the Woodcraft League. The question, then, is this: What was Seton thinking when he joined his vision with that of Baden-Powell?

After reading *Aids to Scouting*, Seton wrote admiringly about it to Baden-Powell in November, adding, "It is exactly the sort of thing that I am trying to carry on in America . . ." But Seton and the general were not trying to create "exactly" the same kind of organization. The general kept Seton informed of the developments of 1907, when Scouting allied itself with newspaper publisher Arthur Pearson, whose publicity for the effort led directly to its massive initial success. Baden-Powell organized an experimental camp for boys, emulating to some degree the first Seton Indian camps of over five years earlier—minus the American Indian theme.

The two founders of Scouting held in common a belief that engaging boys in activities such as camping and outdoor skills inculcated values that led them into productive manhood. The question of authorship of ideas in service of that goal arose as soon as a copy of *Scouting for Boys* reached Seton. Alarmed at what he found, he wrote Baden-Powell in the early part of 1908, expressing his surprise at not having received full credit for his contributions to the new book. Instead of addressing the issue directly, Baden-Powell wrote back in March expressing his regret that "I should have omitted mentioning the source of several of the games," while pointing out those pages on which Seton was credited. In a note inserted into his Baden-Powell file in 1940, referring to the controversy of 1908, Seton wrote that the issue was actually about "the wholesale piracy of my work." At the end of 1909, Seton tried again, complaining to Baden-Powell that the idea of youth camps "in which boys were taught scouting and woodcraft" should have been attributed to him. Seton pointed out that he had given the general credit for his contributions to the seventh Birch Bark Roll. In January, Baden-Powell wrote back, saying that he would include a statement "of my indebtedness to

Tracking iron (fox), 1908. Designed by Seton to strap to the bottom of a shoe; the wearer would make animal tracks for others to practice following. Philmont Museum.

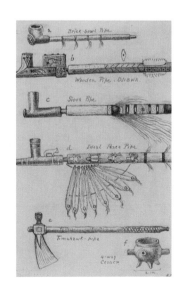

you for several details" in future editions of *Scouting for Boys*, a promise he did not keep. In May 1910, Baden-Powell stated his disagreement with Seton's notions: "it never entered my head that I was going to assist your movement in England." While Baden-Powell did not bring his Boy Scout organization to America, he wrote in his May letter that Seton should expect the idea to find its way over on its own. In fact, it already had, with several organizations gearing up to use variations on the Boy Scout name.

W. D. Boyce, publisher of the *Chicago Ledger* newspaper, first learned about the Boy Scouts during a trip to London. Disoriented and lost in the city's notorious fog, Boyce was approached by a helpful Scout who volunteered to give him directions. Greatly impressed by this courtesy, Boyce wanted to learn about this new organization. He soon found out that in England the Pearson publishing empire had put substantial effort into promoting Scouting. Realizing that newspaper sponsorship of a boys' organization might be successful in the United States, in February 1910, Boyce incorporated a new organization—the Boy Scouts of America—promising it substantial financial support. This support never materialized, and after about three months, Boyce dropped out. (He later started a second Scout organization that eventually merged with the Boy Scouts of America.)

Five days before Seton received Baden-Powell's letter about the Scouts coming to America, Edgar M. Robinson, an executive of the YMCA recruited by Boyce, convened a meeting in New York to make the Boy Scouts of America a viable organization. He had made a career of working for the benefit of boys and clearly saw this new scheme as a promising way to better the lives of youth. He made two significant contributions. First, he took up the administrative reins of the fledgling operation in its first months. And second, he convinced Seton to act as its prime promoter. A small but growing group met on June 21 to formalize its efforts. That day was a pivotal event in the foundation of the Boy Scouts of America. Seton, who agreed with Baden-Powell's assessment about the inevitability of the success of Scouting in the United States, was elected as chair of the Executive Committee. While he wanted to remain relevant to the outdoor youth education movement, that movement also needed him as its most visible proponent. He concentrated his efforts for the next four months on establishing the Scouts in America, as usual doing a lot of things at once (in partnership with Robinson), including recruiting supporters needed to make the organization a success; signing on big-name celebrities in honorary roles (President William Howard Taft as Honorary President, and former president Theodore Roosevelt as Honorary Vice President); raising funds; convincing other nascent Scout groups to merge with the Boy Scouts of America; running the forerunner of the Scout Jamborees, a joint Woodcraft Indian and Boy Scout campout at Silver Bay, New York, in August; and coming up with an organizational scheme for what would become individual troops.

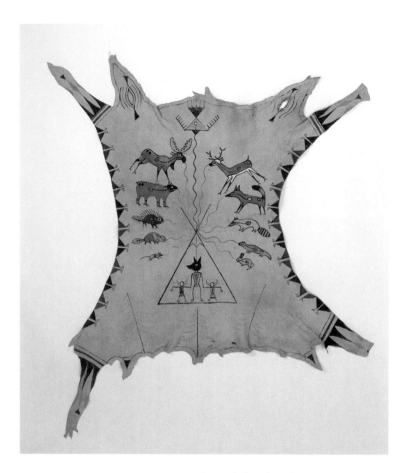

Painted hide, fabricated by Seton, n.d. Philmont Museum. Photo credit: Dave Emery.

Seton's work ensured the success of the fledgling Boy Scouts of America. From the very beginning, however, there were signs of his incompatibility with the organization he was establishing. He soon received an important warning about the course upon which he had embarked. Seton's advisor and mentor, William T. Hornaday, wrote him a letter within days of the first formal organizational meeting of the Boy Scouts, on June 28, 1910.

There is serious work for you to do in retaining the friendship of Dan Beard. Dan has been much annoyed . . . I have told Dan that you do not claim that you "originated the idea" of boy scouts,—as this advertisement [in a magazine] *would have it appear; but that you and Dan are in the same boat, and need to make common cause against a common enemy, who will rob you both of your well-earned credit for what you have done for the boys of America. It will take both of you, standing solidly together, to hold your own against the men who will be quite willing to snow you under, if they can. So far as the boys of America are concerned, the work done by yourself and Dan Beard furnishes glory enough for both of you; and you can each do the other an excellent service as claimant that justice shall be done the other fellow!*

Hornaday's letter is nothing less than startling: just about a week after the important organizational meeting of the Boy Scouts in which Seton had been elected chair, forces had already marshaled to push him out. Seton had lost the war for control of Scouting in America before the first battle. Not named in this revelation by Hornaday are those who sought to get rid of both Seton and Beard. In the event, the two naturalists kept up their feud with one another, and Hornaday's prediction came to pass. Equally alarming is a letter of support for Scouting written to Seton from Roosevelt in September, composed just before Baden-Powell, Seton, and Beard were to attend the first major public event launching the Boy Scout movement in America.

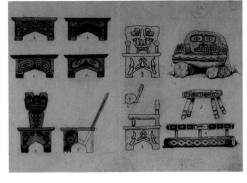

I wish it were possible for me to be at the dinner to-night at which Lt.-Gen. Baden-Powell is to be the guest of honor. I should value greatly the chance to meet General Baden-Powell; and I should value even more the chance to identify myself with so admirable a movement as this—the Boy Scouts of America. I believe in the movement with all my heart. Unfortunately, I simply haven't the time to take an active part therein; but I will gladly accept the honorary Vice-Presidency, as you suggest.

The excessive development of city life in modern industrial civilization which has seen its climax here in our own country, is accompanied by a very unhealthy atrophying of some of the essential virtues which must be embodied in any man who is to be a good soldier, and which especially ought to be embodied in every man to be a really good citizen in time of peace.

Your movement aims at counteracting these unhealthy tendencies. Your especial aim is to make the boys good citizens in time of peace, and incidentally to fit them to become good soldiers in time of war, although the latter inevitably follows, being what might be called a by-product of the former.

I heartily wish all success to the movement.

Roosevelt had got it partly right—Baden-Powell's concept for the Boy Scouts was to create good soldiers. But that was not at all Seton's goal. Did Roosevelt misunderstand Seton? Or was this a warning? Just as Roosevelt had wrecked Seton's career as a naturalist in the Nature Faker controversy (even if inadvertently), the letter indicated that his expectations for the new organization were in line with Baden-Powell's vision.

Meanwhile, Seton made an attempt at reconciliation with Baden-Powell. The Boy Scouts held a grand dinner for the general in New York, celebrating at the same time the creation of their organization. Seton hosted the event in a ballroom of the Waldorf Astoria, where he praised the Hero of Mafeking, introducing Baden-Powell as the father of Scouting. The general was magnanimous in his response: "You have made a mistake, Mr. Seton, in your remarks to the effect that I am the father of this idea of Scouting for boys. I may say that you are the father of it, or that Dan Beard is the father. I am only one of the uncles, I might say." The expressions of good feelings that night amounted to little more than a temporary truce among the three strong-willed men, a truce that held throughout the first critical months in the formation of the Boy Scouts of America.

During that time, Seton made an enduring contribution to the Scouting movement by helping create the first Scout handbook for boys (referred to as the "original edition"). Credited jointly to both Seton and Baden-Powell, since it combined parts of the Birch

The three founders of the
world Scouting movement
posed for their only
photograph together in
New York City, September
23, 1910. Library and
Archives Canada.

Bark Roll and *Scouting for Boys*, the handbook served as a model for many outdoor skills books over the next century. The following year, under different editors, the Boy Scouts brought out a second handbook—referred to as the "1st edition"—that was more closely modeled on its English counterpart. The Boy Scouts of America *Handbook for Boys* was first printed for limited release with 4,200 copies in June 1911. The subject matter of the book, including contributions by Seton, was arranged haphazardly. Despite its lack of apparent organization, the next printing of the handbook proved extraordinarily popular, selling out its 70,000 copies in a short time. In the decades that followed, various editions of the *Boy Scout Handbook* built up an enviable sales record—more than seven million copies have been printed over the course of a century. Seton's name was dropped from the publication early on, but of all his accomplishments, launching the *Boy Scout Handbook* tradition is one of the more notable.

Seton wrote an introduction to the "1st edition" of the *Boy Scout Handbook*, an essay—about himself! As he had done earlier in *Two Little Savages*, he referred to a boy who once upon a time had a burning desire to know the names of animals and plants, who wanted to know everything about camping and survival in nature, and who had more than just a little feeling of romance for the outdoor life. He continued, "Young Scouts of America, that boy is writing to you now." He promised that the Scouting program would

"Seton's own Boy Scout Troop," 1915. The intriguing caption on the photograph suggests that Seton may have been a Scoutmaster. Library and Archives Canada

make a boy at home not just in the wilderness, but in town as well, through the skills of "Life-craft" and "Wood-craft." A Scout could pick up a wide range of knowledge, from swimming and first aid to forestry and photography. He asked, "Do you believe in loyalty, courage, and kindness? Would you like to get habits that surely make your success in life?" And he concluded, "This is, indeed, the book that I so longed for, in those far-off days when I wandered, heart hungry in the woods." The handbook could be criticized for what it left out, for poor illustrations and less-than-stellar editing. But it was a start, an introduction to a lifetime of outdoor activity, good health, and moral direction. If that sounds a little too grand in a more cynical age, then there were also sections with information not often thought about today, such as how to stop runaway horses (don't wave your arm in front of the animal) or what to do about a mad dog (kill it at once!).

The attitude toward mad dogs was taken up by members of the Executive Committee and applied to Seton. The details of what happened remain fuzzy, but somehow, when a permanent Executive Committee was formed in the fall of 1910, as Hornaday had warned, Seton was written out of the command structure and given the honorary, powerless position of Chief Scout. At this same time, Edgar Robinson left the Scouts to return to the YMCA. A new Scout administrator, James E. West, a lawyer for whom Seton had not a shred of respect, replaced Robinson. Complicating matters, in the summer of 1910, Dan Beard sided against Seton as often as he could, jealous of Seton's accomplishments. For his trouble, Beard was given the honorary, equally powerless position of National Scout Commissioner. This worked well for West, who in his first weeks largely maneuvered the two American founders of Scouting out of any role in the organization other than serving as publicists.

West was the ultimate organization man, with good political connections stemming in part from his activism on children's judicial issues. If Seton and Beard disliked one another for having too much in common, Seton and West hated one another for having nothing in common. Seton felt that the plodding, straight-arrow bureaucrat wanted to kill every spark of spontaneity and creativity that should be the very heart of youth education. While "Uncle" Dan Beard thrilled boys by showing them how to throw a tomahawk and Seton enchanted them with stories about Lobo and Indians, the methodical West was not known for his charisma. But from an institutional standpoint, he was exactly what the Scouts needed. Seton had started an organization without central administration. Beard had started one with no substantial basis, and Baden-Powell had envisioned yet another as an adjunct to the British Army. West took a different tack. He oversaw Scouting's expansion into an organization of hundreds of thousands of boys formed into long-lasting local troops. He firmed up the finances of what was, after all, an experimental organization when it started. He fiercely protected and fought for the reputation of the organization, upholding its rights to the name Boy Scouts. He molded the organization into conformity with his vision for over thirty years. And as his final revenge against the hated Seton, at the end of his tenure, he had himself named Chief Scout, a title that was to have been exclusively reserved for Seton. For decades after West's retirement, the Boy Scouts of America has continued to build upon organizational structures first built by West. Even Seton grudgingly admitted that West was a superb administrator.

As Seton unsuccessfully struggled during the next three years to maintain his influence in Scouting, he did something truly remarkable. He continued to devote his Herculean energies to the benefit of its boy members. Seton, in his unending travels, promoted Scouting despite his reservations about West and the organization's favoring Baden-Powell's philosophy over his own. He did so because he could see that the benefit to boys—and to such a great number of boys—was worth a great deal of personal sacrifice. Seton's heart overcame his egocentric, self-promoter persona to carry on his support for Scouting far longer than was good for him personally. Many of his Woodcraft ideals, such as respect for nature and using the outdoors as a platform for finding one's values, survived within Scouting because of his tenacity. Millions of boys and girls have been introduced to conservation, wilderness, wildlife protection, woodcraft, camping, Indian lore, and environmental education through Scouting, and Scouting came to honor these values through Seton.

Seton's friends may have worried about him and the ongoing deterioration of his relationship with the Scouts. Hornaday tried to persuade him to return to natural history and conservation. His publisher Frank Doubleday stated the obvious, that both Seton and the Boy Scouts would benefit by his departure. Seton threatened to resign, but he didn't follow through.

Then an event occurred that changed everything. In Europe, in June 1914, a Serb assassinated the archduke who was heir to the Austro-Hungarian throne, soon leading to the outbreak of a terrible war in Europe, the disintegration of the Austro-Hungarian Empire, and eventually a rearrangement of continental borders. This did not at first seem to have much to do with the Boy Scouts of America, but it proved the final death knell for Woodcraft as the philosophy guiding Scouting. In the ideological struggle between the Seton model of local social responsibility and individual achievement and the Baden-Powell model of national patriotism and sacrifice for the state, the latter won out. America, it seemed, although not without controversy, was not only a great power, but *the* great power, and with its new role in the world came vast and uncharted responsibilities. The twentieth century of course became the American Century, one of global wars that a global power, no matter how reluctant, could not avoid, and America inevitably took its part in resolving the European mess. Seton was perceived as being on the wrong side, in support of antiwar sentiment, summarized as a pacifist. Theodore Roosevelt called an individual of this persuasion a "sissy." Behind the scenes, Roosevelt lumped Seton into this group, and he shared that opinion in a letter to West.

If ever anyone did not deserve the label of pacifist or sissy, it was Seton, but Roosevelt's labeling of Seton as an antiwar activist trumped all other perceptions of him. Seton volunteered to serve in the British military—hardly the action of a pacifist—but was turned down due to his age (fifty-four). Seton had already begun his withdrawal from Scouting, deciding to miss the annual meeting in February 1915, Scouting's fifth anniversary. With Seton absent, the managing directors of the Boy Scouts chose not to continue the position of Chief Scout. But Seton's lower profile was still not low enough. In November, Roosevelt wrote West that he expected the Boy Scouts would take the right steps to prepare their membership for military service and that the organization's leaders could not afford to associate themselves with anyone who thought otherwise. By now, Seton's objection to Baden-Powell–style militarism was no secret; Roosevelt's letter apparently referred to Seton, who was generally skeptical of war as a legitimate means of settling disputes. Seton did not object to British or American participation in this particular war;

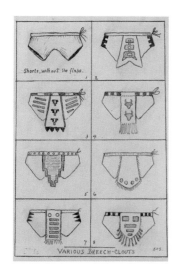

nonetheless, he felt that warfare was the concern of adults, not of children. For Roosevelt, the view that children should not be made "eager and ready to fight" was unpatriotic.

The Boy Scouts had other issues with Seton as well: he was not an American but a citizen of Great Britain. Seton seemed to be unaware of the symbolic importance of citizenship to the Americans, while at the same time British citizenship remained important to him. It was also not lost on the male Republican Scout leadership that Grace Gallatin Seton was in the forefront of the suffragette movement, a substantial irritant for them. If they bothered reading it, they would also have objected to Seton's 1913 essay, "The Spartans of the West," in which Seton wrote about the nobility of the American Indian and the superiority of traditional "Red" culture over that created by the white man. He also criticized the American government for the terrible treatment meted out to its native citizens.

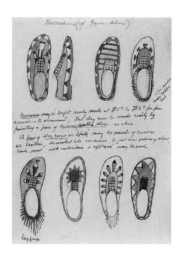

The final nail in the coffin of Seton's dealings with Scouting came not from West but from Dan Beard. Although Beard had not been treated any better by West than had Seton, he wanted more than anything to force Seton out of the organization, and by chance or design he finally found a way to do so. In November 1915, just before Roosevelt sent his letter to West, Beard claimed in an interview to have originated the Boy Scouts all by himself. The claim was ludicrous, and it earned him letters from both Seton and Grace, asking him not to go public with his claims. Uncle Dan responded with a nasty note.

[no salutation]

O come off, Seton: don't make a fool of yourself. Not interested in the dates. Have no knowledge of the articles to which you refer. Have neither power nor desire to muzzle press. You make me tired. Not guilty!

If you really want to fight, would suggest that you will be welcomed in the trenches as "ENGLAND EXPECTS ALL LOYAL SONS TO DO THEIR DUTY!"

Please let us close the incident.

There is no record of Seton's response to Beard's letter, but since he had attempted to enlist in the military, he must have been enraged beyond all measure. It is unlikely that Seton knew about the Roosevelt letter, although if he had known, this would have made the situation for him much worse. But after Beard's letter, his official dealings with the Scouts quickly came to an end. The cumulative effect of seven years of disappointments, beginning with what he saw as Baden-Powell's plagiarism, Beard's provocations, and fights with West and the Executive Board, was that Seton flew into a rage. He called a news conference, inviting reporters to his Fifth Avenue apartment to announce his

final departure from Scouting. He timed his announcement to coincide with a major Boy Scout event in which the organization planned to raise $200,000 in four days, an astonishing amount of money for that period. Attesting to Seton's celebrity, his announcement ran above that of the fund-raiser—his headline large, that of the Boy Scouts a mere subheading below his story. He also gave the reporters his most memorable quote, a summary, as he saw it, of the developments of the youth movement from 1902 to 1915: "Seton started it; Baden-Powell boomed it; West killed it." He continued:

I sent my resignation as head of the Boy Scouts some months ago, but the organization has not acted upon it. I don't know why nothing has been done, but I do feel that the organization is not acting fairly either toward me or the public in allowing the public to suppose that they are still deriving their inspiration from me. It should be clearly stated and I want it understood, that I esteem the Executive Board of the Boy Scouts to be a splendid lot of men, giving freely of their time and money to the work. My only criticism is that they have allowed all direction and power to centre in the hands of James E. West, a lawyer who is a man of great executive ability but without knowledge of the activities of boys; who has no point of contact with boys, and who, I might almost say, has never seen the blue sky in his life.

I wanted good naturedly to resign from the Boy Scouts, but they still have my name on their papers, and I hear from people all over the country who still think that I am connected with the Boy Scouts. I bought yesterday a copy of the handbook of the organization, and in it is printed an introduction signed by me as Chief Scout. I was Chief Scout up to last February, but after that I resigned.

I intend to resign from many things in order to concentrate my activities on the Woodcraft League, which best gives my message to the world.

West must have seen it differently—whatever else he was getting from Seton, it wasn't inspiration. He was the target of a man whose popularity he could never hope to rival, but, his fund-raising plan at risk, he counterattacked in the *New York Times* the very next day. He began with a quote misrepresenting one of Seton's friends as having turned against him, under the headline "West Says Seton Is Not a Patriot."

As stated by Dr. William T. Hornaday of the New York Zoological Society, in the appeal in the present campaign, "The Boy Scouts movement is a great national antidote for the devilish spirit of anarchy to the states and nation that is now cropping up like rank and poisonous weeds all along the path of our nation's progress." When it was discovered that Mr. Seton was in harmony with the views of anarchists and radical socialists on the question of whether the Boy Scouts of America should stand for patriotism and good citizenship, no time was lost in developing the issue.

JACK
IN
A
PULPIT

Mr. Seton was given a reasonable, fair opportunity to make himself clear on this subject, but he hedged and stated that he could not make a definite promise that he would ever become a citizen of the United States.

Indeed, he went further and repeated the objection to the Boy Scout Handbook, including a chapter on "Patriotism," and contended that the Boy Scouts of America should not undertake to have boys pledging allegiance to their country, but leave them free to support our country when they thought our country was right and to damn it when they thought it was wrong. He personally made clear that he damned our country for most of its past history. This is the real and only reason that Mr. Seton is not now Chief Scout of the Boy Scouts of America.

When shown this statement Mr. Seton said:

"You notice that Mr. West does not reply to any of my statements, but contents himself with calling me an anarchist and a Socialist. It is quite the first time in my life that any one has taken such a view of me. Not long ago West accused me of being a 'monarchist,' and said I was too 'autocratic.' If the Boy Scout Board will look up my letter they will find that in the same paragraph in which I criticise America for the Mexican wars I was still more severe on England for the Chinese opium war. In other words, I was denouncing all aggressive warfare. I am sorry to learn that the Chief Scout Executive approves such things.

"The case is very clear. First, I am not in sympathy with the present trend of the Boy Scout movement; second, I think I have a national message to deliver; and third, I can deliver that message best through the Woodcraft League. Henceforth, I shall focus my activities on that work."

An unattributed article in the January *Boys' Life*, "Why Mr. Seton Is Not Chief Scout," claimed that Scouting would not be affected by his departure from the organization and that as regarded authorship of the *Boy Scout Handbook*, Seton had "contributed nothing essential to the program of Scouting" and that any of his sections in the book could in the future be replaced by the work of "eminent American citizens." In the meantime, Seton had withdrawn from the battle and founded the Woodcraft League in December 1915. In June 1916, the Congress of the United States granted to the Boy Scouts of America a federal charter, which included a provision stating that members of the organization must be American citizens.

Cardinal Flower

Message to the World

The eleventh edition of the Birch Bark Roll came out in 1913 with the title *The Book of Woodcraft and Indian Lore.* At 567 pages, and including more than five hundred drawings, it was by far the most ambitious work ever published about outdoor recreation. It also combined nature study and forestry with stories about Indians, showing totems and teepee designs along with games for campers. Most of all, Woodcraft was about a set of values—Lifecraft, as Seton called it, or guidance for the transition between childhood and adulthood. (This book was supplemented by the important 1915 *Manual of the Woodcraft Indians*.) The 1913 edition, which in many chapter headings substituted "Scouting" for "Woodcraft," came about because of the difficulties Seton faced in keeping his ideas within the Boy Scouts' *Handbook for Boys*. The 1915 manual became his most formal statement to date about the Woodcraft organization itself. It specified Woodcraft programs by age group: the Little Lodge for children, the Big Lodge for boys, and the Red Lodge for adults. The Red Lodge had its own laws that were not made public—including requirements so severe concerning sign language, outdoor lore, and other subjects that no one but Seton himself could possibly have mastered them all. The Red Lodge disappeared within a few years, but the Woodcraft League of

Seton with Woodcraft League parade float, possibly in Connecticut, ca. 1916. Historical Society of the Town of Greenwich.

America continued its existence through Seton's move back to New Mexico in 1930, after which it gradually faded away.

The Woodcraft League had largely been an organization of the northeastern states, and Seton's departure from that part of the country marked its death knell. His friend Hamlin Garland had foreseen this years earlier, in the lead up to World War I:

> *As I sat through Seton's ceremony so suggestive of the outdoor life, I could not put aside a sense of the fact that it all sprang from him and that when he dropped out the League would end. The Boy Scouts, a rival organization, is more in harmony with the growing war spirit and less dependent on any one personality.*

Just as telling, a cause for the demise of the organization is found in Seton's own words to his longtime colleague, Frank Chapman, which clearly show that Seton was a brilliant conceptualist, but less talented as an administrator.

Seton in aboriginal dress, ca. 1915. Library and Archives Canada.

> *Concerning the Woodcraft League, I guess you realize that my dream was to make it a movement rather than an organization. Nevertheless, the organization was forced on me by my friends. Our program has been adopted by the numerous organizations that have followed after. The Woodcraft is, as you know, the oldest. Although its formal announcement was 1902, I had it in good shape in 1898 as an idea.*
>
> *How many members are there in it? It is so loosely organized that I am not sure. But I should say about 10,000 are using the program as it was offered by me. But every camp in the country—and there are about 28,000 of them—is using the program in some measure. This applies not only to America, but to Canada, England, Europe, Australia, and even Asia. At least a million young people use it.*

In *Lives of Game Animals*, Seton wrote that "While following zoological studies myself, I was not forgetful of the boys who wanted the very thing that I had so hungered for as a child . . . I was in some degree responsible for keeping alive in them a love of outdoor life and animals." But it was much more than that. The development of his philosophy continued through the 1927 edition of the Birch Bark Roll and two pamphlets with three essays from 1928, *Blazes on the Trail*. In the essay "No. 1 Lifecraft Or Woodcraft,

Above left: Seton dancing at DeWinton, 1920s, Library and Archives Canada.

Above right: Seton with girls' group, 1920s. Historical Society of the Town of Greenwich, Connecticut.

The Four-Fold Way," Seton gave an account of how he came to create the Woodcraft movement, starting with his search for an ideal of manhood:

I had a vision for my people,—a man of perfect manhood, a being physically robust, an athlete, an outdoors man, accustomed to brunt of flood, wind and sun—rough road and open spaces—a man wise in the way of the woods, sagacious in council, dignified, courteous, respectful to all, and kindly as a good-natured giant; a man whose life was clean, picturesque, heroic and unsordid, a man of courage, equipped for emergencies, possessing his soul at all times, and filled with a religion that consists, not of mere occasional observances, not of vague merits hoarded in the skies, but of a strong kind of spirit that makes him desired and helpful here today.

Having found in the native peoples of North America a continental society that exhibited this high standard of morality, Seton felt compelled to teach those values to American youth. Always anti-authoritarian, he denounced the "Compulsionists, who believe that all boys are born bad, the children of the devil." According to Seton, this group believed in repression of natural instincts and punishment-driven behavior

Clockwise from top left: Seton with girls' group, 1920s. Historical Society of the Town of Greenwich.

Metal drum with Woodcraft symbols painted on hide by Seton, n.d. Academy for the Love of Learning.

Chest, incised and stained by Seton, with carved handles and feet, ca. 1910. Philmont Museum. Photo credit: Dave Emery.

Seton demonstrating cooking, 1920s. Academy for the Love of Learning.

modification, an approach he assigned to "militarists" and conservative religious people such as his own parents. He put himself in the camp of the "Developmentalists, who believe that all boys (with rare exceptions) are born good, are the children of God, and need only to be developed under sound leadership. Of this class are the Woodcrafters." In this approach, children's instincts are acknowledged, their behavior guided rather than forced into appropriate directions. Teenagers are sometimes required to be "reformed," but only after having been "deformed" to begin with. By the time juveniles had to be jailed—a punishment that didn't help the child in any event—the adults in their lives had already clearly failed them. Children could be more successfully raised by giving them an opportunity to experience wild nature while learning at the same time about the self-sufficiency needed for a life (or even visits) close to the land. *Two Little Savages*, the Birch Bark Roll series, and a novel set in 1812, *Rolf in the Woods*, about an adventurous young man, provided practical guidance as well as entertainment. These publications recognized "instinct" in youth—the life forces in an individual seeking growth and experience through play (at an early age), through association with age-peers in "gangs" (at an older age), and, later still, at sixteen and older, through seeking individual identity in intellectual, sexual, and spiritual matters. There was nothing very original about this; Seton's thinking reflected the intellectual currents of the Progressive Era. His concern for youth was, however, genuine, and his contribution as an educator to keep children from being "deformed" in the first place was original. Seton proposed outdoor recreation in which children of both sexes could manage their own fun—with adult guidance and support and participation from the family. His philosophy was one of optimism.

> *Our watchword is "Blue Sky." For under the blue sky, in the sunlight, we seek to live our lives; and our thoughts are of "blue sky," for that means "cheer"; and when there are clouds, we know that the blue sky is ever behind them, and will come again.*

CHAPTER FIVE

New Mexico, Part Two

Grace Gallatin Seton-Thompson (as she was known in 1901) was, like her husband, a multitalented and complex person. In her lifetime she became a women's rights activist, a travel writer, an international adventurer, a big-game hunter, and a lecturer. Born in California, raised and educated in New York City after age nine, and privileged with occasional trips to Paris, she grew up sophisticated and well connected. The connections and introductions likely proved of great significance to her ambitious husband.

Of Grace's many accomplishments, one of her most significant was the co-creation of her husband's career as a best-selling author. She pushed him to put together and sell the projects that became *Wild Animals I Have Known* and *The Trail of the Sandhill Stag*, and over the course of several books she helped with the design and overall treatment. She also served for many years as his publicist and business manager, holding together the details of his business life so that he could concentrate on creative writing.

This beneficial partnership continued when Grace signed on as an early supporter of Seton's Woodcraft movement. From 1902 onward, she put up with her husband spending his summers as a boy playing Indian, but, more than that, she took an active role in the early camps. Late in his life, Leonard S. Clark, one of the first Seton Indians

Right: "Greetings from the Setons to You and Yours," ink, 1919. Academy for the Love of Learning.

Facing, top: *Peace River*, ink, 1920s. Academy for the Love of Learning.

Facing, bottom: *The Desert Hush*, ink, 1920s. Academy for the Love of Learning.

PEACE RIVER. E.T. SETON.

The Desert Hush. E.T. SETON.

and one of Seton's most ardent supporters, recalled Grace's contributions: "You can't give Mr. Seton all the glory. Mrs. Seton was a wonderful, wonderful woman. She used to come over to the camp fire. If a boy hurt himself a little bit, it was Mrs. Seton who would bind up his cut finger . . . She was a tremendous woman and a tremendous help." Grace was instrumental in finding a permanent home for Woodcraft philosophy in the Campfire Girls (now Camp Fire USA), founded in 1910 by Luther and Charlotte Gulick. According to Grace Seton's biographer, Lucinda H. MacKethan, the organization had a strong grounding in Woodcraft.

MacKethan points out that for many years Seton and Grace "were a team in every endeavor." Grace enjoyed travel and adventure as much as her husband—the two of them were constantly on the move, together or separately. The city girl proved exceptionally adroit at taking on any challenge and facing any danger. Her two books about her Western travels with her husband, *A Woman Tenderfoot* (1900) and *Nimrod's Wife* (1907), were written with verve and humor, further enhancing Seton's reputation as a celebrity, as well as creating her own public identity. At the same time, Seton was away from her much of the time. The demands of the lecture circuit made him an incessant traveler. Frequent and sometimes lengthy separations must have put great strain on their marriage. Grace lived actively in his absence, taking a leading role as a suffragist in Connecticut and, during World War I, financing an ambulance unit in France. By the end of the war, she began a life of independent foreign travel to research her books. The couple spent increasingly less time together until by 1922 they were, according to MacKethan, "more or less completely separated."

The Setons' relationship reached a major milestone in 1925 when they signed a separation agreement in Connecticut. Grace seemed reconciled to maintaining this arrangement and so was deeply hurt when, in 1934, Seton obtained a divorce from her in a Mexican court. This action apparently had no standing in an American court, but it did force Grace to come to a settlement with her husband. A final divorce decree was entered into the records of the First Judicial District, Santa Fe, New Mexico, on January 18, 1935.

Thus ended a partnership going back forty-one years to when, as a young woman, Grace met Seton, more than eleven years older, on the fateful voyage to Paris.

Grace published five more travel books, the last one in 1938, always emphasizing the status of women. Although they sold in only modest amounts, her books did receive recognition: in 1926 her book on India, *Yes, Lady Saheb: A Woman's Adventurings with Mysterious India,* was selected by the National League of American Pen Women as the best book of the year, and in 1933 her book on Egypt, *A Woman Tenderfoot in Egypt,* was chosen by the Century of Progress Exhibition as one of the best hundred books

Desert camp, near Las Vegas, New Mexico, August 3, 1927. Library and Archives Canada.

by American women. In her later years she studied mysticism and Eastern religions intensively, and she also wrote poetry, much of it about her travels, which she published in two slim volumes. As the years went on, she watched with pride as her daughter began producing her best-selling novels— seven of them during Grace's lifetime. (Grace died in 1959 at the age of eighty-seven.)

Ann, the Setons' only child, was born in their winter apartment in Manhattan on January 23, 1904, and was first taken to Wyndygoul in the spring of that year. She grew up amid the unending restlessness of her two parents. At the end of 1914, and again in August of 1915, she accompanied them on trips to New Mexico, visiting Indian pueblos and the artist colonies of Taos and Santa Fe, among other places. Those trips were among her few opportunities to spend time with her father; he was so often away from home that she did not have the chance to establish a close relationship with him. When Seton and Grace finally divorced, the separation affected Ann as well; she rarely saw Seton after his move to New Mexico. In the divorce settlement, Seton had to give to Grace all rights to his literary and artistic properties, excepting *Lives of Game Animals*. In return, Grace gave up any claim on the New Mexico property he had purchased while still married to her. (New Mexico was, and is, a community property state.) In his will, Seton gave nearly everything to his second wife, Julia, leaving Ann with a longing for paternal love that could only be realized by the characters she brought to life in her fiction, as MacKethan points out:

> *In* [Ann's novels], *we meet several romantic father-widowers who are deeply attached to their daughters. . . . These works, often praised for the detailed historical research that went into them, can also be examined for the complex psychology that the author built into her characters, a psychology charged with compulsions and conflicts related to her own upbringing.*

Following her father's lead, Ann later changed her name, to Anya. She had acquired her parents' skill as a writer, and she ended up selling more books than both of them combined, with ten best-selling novels published between 1941 and 1973. She died in 1990.

Around 1922, Seton took up with Julia Moss Buttree, whom he had met a few years earlier. The intimate details of their private lives are not documented, although early on Ann suspected that Julia was pursuing her father, even though both Julia and Ernest were married to other partners. Julia—who was usually called "Julie"—described her first meeting with Seton (at one of his lectures) in the rhapsodic terms of a romance novel: "When the first words came through his lips, an electric thrill went through me . . . I fell under the spell of the narrative. Yet, when the speaker ceased, I realized that I had not taken in the end of the story—I had been wholly lost in the cadence of his voice." The attraction was mutual and unapologetic, notwithstanding Julia being almost three decades younger than Seton. They met after the lecture, touched hands, and Seton told her, "My, we could have a lot of fun together." And apparently they did, for almost a quarter century, ending only with his death. Soon after their meeting, Julia would take up work as Seton's secretary and personal assistant. She had already earned degrees in classical languages and drama, and she soon developed an interest in youth education and Indian lore. She was smart and organized, the perfect support for Seton during the years he spent on *Lives of Game Animals*.

In 1923, Seton abandoned the large house at DeWinton in Greenwich (successor to the one at Wyndygoul) for a smaller house called Little Peequo, on his property adjoining DeWinton, where he and Julia worked together nearly constantly. Eventually, the two lived more or less openly together. The views of Julia's husband, Ted Buttree, have not found their way into the historical record, although the relationship between Seton and Buttree seems to have been cordial, with Seton even setting Buttree up in a small business (a tea room). And when Seton and Julia moved to New Mexico, Buttree—and his new girlfriend—moved with them. The two couples even shared a house together for a time at the newly built Seton Village. This arrangement might have seemed extraordinary anywhere else, but in the interwar years, the Anglo art colonies of Santa Fe and Taos were places where social and sexual experimentation among artists and writers was, if not common, then at least not exceptional. From Seton's standpoint, Julia was important to him both for the interests they shared and because in her he found a woman to keep him on track with his projects as he entered the final phase of his life.

On the Last Rampart of the Rockies

From the Brooks Range in Alaska, the Rocky Mountains spread southward three thousand miles to the Sangre de Cristo Range in New Mexico. Determining the exact southern terminus of the entire chain may not be possible, but it was on one of its final

Seton and Julia in front of their teepee, New Mexico, 1927. Academy for the Love of Learning.

spurs that Seton built his last home. In his autobiography, he called the place a rampart; the building on the outcrop of red granite eventually came to be called Seton Castle. It was here that he made his last stand.

Seton and Julia's contemplation of a move to New Mexico occurred while they were still at work finishing *Lives of Game Animals*. They traveled to Santa Fe in 1927 and then twice in each of the succeeding years in search of the perfect property. They spent two months in New Mexico on the first trip, limiting their search to a hundred miles in every direction from Santa Fe. The property they found by September 1929 was only about six miles by road from the center of the capital city. At nearly 2,500 acres, it was larger than they needed, and there were no improvements on the entire tract, but it was a good investment. They made an offer in February of the following year. Julia recalled, "We knew at once that this was the spot we had been seeking; and on Washington's birthday that year, we two camped out on the property." The land offered unparalleled views and, even more important, to their perception, a sense of deep spirituality. It was this feeling that had attracted the two of them to Santa Fe from the beginning. They tramped the grounds together searching for the spot on which to locate their home—and their lives—for all their remaining years. They could not come

to a decision until they came upon the last rampart of the Rockies where, Julia wrote, they found wisdom higher than their own—or perhaps it found them.

> *But when we stood together one memorable evening and faced a sunset of unspeakable light, we knew—as we always have known in moments of acceptive decision . . . Everything that we had sought together through the years was there in fullest abundance. Every theory of life that we had held was waiting there to prove its truth and rightness, unvoiced but chanting its alleluia to our grateful hearts. The veil is very thin across this point of view.*

During the summer of 1930 they had a well dug and built a small adobe house named "Yek Yek"—Seton's interpretation of the barking sound made by prairie dogs. The structure sat at the southwest end of what would later become the plaza, or central open area, of Seton Village. At the same time, they began work on the Castle, although, because of its size, it would not be completed for several years. They built at the west end of Seton Village a smaller house called Lagunita, Spanish for "little lake." There were neither lakes nor running streams anywhere nearby, so the term may have been an ironic gesture recognizing the new well; its small production of water had proved a great disappointment. In addition to providing the Setons a place to live while the Castle was under construction, Lagunita served as a model for Seton to try out his architectural ideas on a relatively small scale before translating them into the design of the Castle.

The plumbing in Lagunita was rustic, and electricity was nonexistent the first winter. Over the next two years they constructed several more buildings from stones and adobe bricks, and, in addition, brought in abandoned buildings from the nearby railroad line (purchased from the Santa Fe Railroad for twenty-five dollars) and even old Pullman cars and a caboose that became the interiors around which larger buildings were constructed. None of the buildings were well heated, so although the summer

population grew over the following years, Seton Village was all but abandoned during most winters. Seton and Julia spent the cold seasons in Texas, California, or Mexico.

The Castle finally reached a habitable stage in April 1934, although, like the rest of the Seton Village buildings, it best lent itself to three-season occupation. Seton was delighted with his new building, which was ready just in time for the third season of the College of Indian Wisdom, a program of The Woodcraft League of America, Inc. The college was an academically accredited training program for adults, run on Seton's property, in conjunction with a summer camp for children. Attendees could get both theoretical training and on-the-job training, as explained in the brochure:

> *For camp directors, camp counselors, leaders of all outdoors and indoors recreational organizations, playground leaders, teachers of handicrafts, teachers of Indian schools, etc., or those aspiring to be such . . .*
>
> *The courses emphasize Indian thought throughout, selecting the best ideals of the best Redmen of the past and present. A number of the members of the staff are Indians of the highest attainment in crafts, etc. . . .*
>
> *All instruction is of a practical nature, every member taking an active part. There is very little straight lecturing, except where necessary for academic requirements.*

Each evening, students participated in Woodcraft games and Indian dancing, and, on one evening a week, they traveled to Santa Fe to watch Indian dancers performing at the La Fonda Hotel, located just off the Plaza. Field trips took the students to ancestral Puebloan sites, including Chaco Canyon in the extremely remote northwestern corner of New Mexico. Students also visited Taos Pueblo and other Indian villages to learn about contemporary native culture. There were nine courses to choose from; thirty-five hours of work earned a student one hour of college credit. In keeping with Woodcraft philosophy,

Above left: Prayerful Seton at Woodcraft meeting, ca. 1930s. Library and Archives Canada.

Above right: Lagunita, the first completed house at Seton Village, ca. 1950. Academy for the Love of Learning.

Right: *Seton Institute & Grounds*, watercolor, ink, and colored pencil, 1937. Academy for the Love of Learning.

Below: Seton Castle with farolitos, west façade, ca. 1960s. Photo Archives/ Palace of the Governors.

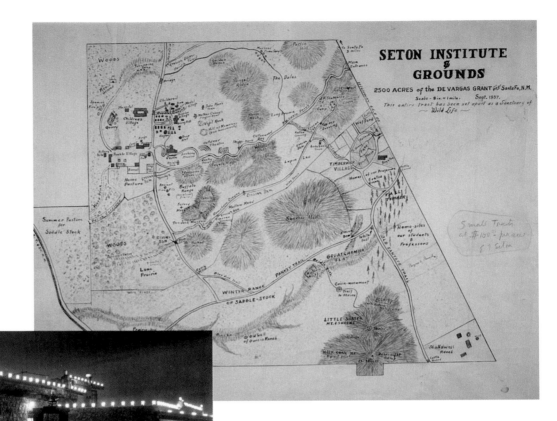

students were taught how to make their own artifacts based on native material culture, with the idea that they would be able to teach these practices back at their home camps. The Art II course, for example, featured "Combination Indian Crafts, including Wool Embroidery, Loom Beading, Elks' Teeth, Beaded Rosettes, Peace Pipes, Katchinas, Spatter Prints, Smoke Prints, Mexican Sandals, Basketry, Councils." In Indian Science, students could learn about the use of plants for food, medicine, and dyes, in addition to sign language and "Animal Imitations." For the academically inclined, there was a course in Indian philosophy and legends. And for the artistic, courses in Indian dancing and Indian music were offered. Teachers included Seton's Indian friends from the pueblos of San Ildefonso and Santa Clara. Anglo stalwarts of the Santa Fe artist colony became involved as well. Ina Sizer Cassidy, a writer as well as wife of painter Gerald Cassidy, and a Santa Fe resident since 1912, taught Indian basketry. (The Cassidys were close friends of the Setons.) Kenneth Chapman, an artist and archaeologist, taught traditional pottery design. Tuition in the mid-1930s cost thirty-five dollars for the first week, discounted for subsequent weeks. Students could rent anything from houses to blankets if they wished.

Clockwise from top left: Like other New Mexico artists of his time, Seton gathered a personal collection of Indian artifacts, including Ojibwa quill work, a Paiute water jar, a Cochiti drum, and a Cherokee basket.

Summers around the Castle were very busy for Seton and Julia, with a staff of forty and up to two hundred students. Simultaneously, they ran the Seton Village Children's Camp, a small operation with only thirty children present at any one time. The camp was located near the "Kiva," a ceremonial building replicating religious structures at the Indian pueblos. The building had been authentically designed by Seton based on observations he had personally made: tribal members at the Taos and San Ildefonso pueblos had invited him into their kivas, an extremely rare privilege for any white person, and an indication that Indian elders held him in respect. Children at Seton's camp slept in log or adobe buildings and occasionally in a teepee. They sang Zuni songs each morning and evening to welcome and then close out the day. As with the original Seton Indians, these campers also made and wore their own Indian costumes and practiced Indian dances. They were proud of the food they prepared, an example of Woodcraft self-reliance: "We raise most of our own vegetables; what we do not raise ourselves, we buy from neighboring farms." Children and adults were invited into Seton's library, the great room of the Castle, once a week to hear Seton tell his stories, after which the young people left while the older ones remained. (Unfortunately, the subjects of their discussions were not recorded.) One of the child campers, Dieter Rall, who attended sessions from 1937 to 1938, recalled that Seton "was a big man—he moved a lot" as he was telling stories, constantly walking back and forth in front of

Clockwise from top left:
Animal Forms—Chiefly Pueblo,
ink, 1920s. Academy for
the Love of Learning.

*Conventional Birds, Pueblo
Designs*, ink, 1920s.
Academy for the Love of
Learning.

Untitled musical
instruments, ink, 1920s.
Academy for the Love of
Learning.

Skull and Buttons, ink, 1920s.
Academy for the Love of
Learning.

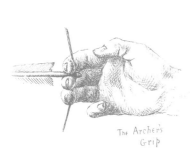

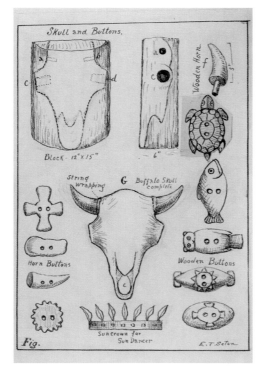

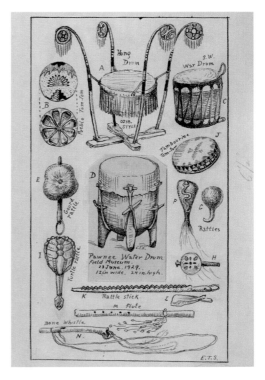

the audience as he warmed up to them. Seton could become so moved by his own stories that "tears would come to his eyes." He told the children that he was especially remorseful over his killing of a moose long ago. He always set their "imaginations racing."

When not involved with the summer programs, Seton and Julia stayed occupied with their lecture tours and bookselling. They published promotional brochures offering single lectures by Julia such as "The Singing Indian," with five changes of costume; "Wild Animals I Have Known" by Seton, concluding with the story of the "giant wolf," Lobo; and joint presentations by both about Indians they had known. As Seton's book royalties declined, the lectures became one of their main sources of income, although the amount they made was little more than their travel expenses. The last major tour in Europe (1936–37) included thirty-five lectures in Great Britain on thirty-five successive nights, followed by appearances in Bonn and Prague. The Woodcraft movement had a small but enthusiastic following among the Czechs. (It survived fascism and communism, continuing into the current century.) Wherever they went, they always carried with them books for sale. While Seton had not written a best-selling book for a long time, selling directly to customers at lectures, as well as by mail order, had its advantages.

Seton repackaged a few old titles—Lobo and Bingo made their return in 1930—but also of importance was that Julia had brought about the establishment of the Seton Village Press. While she and Seton were on one of their many lecture tours, they had met a young couple, Maurice and Marceil Taylor. Maurice had come to hear the "Chief" (as Seton was known in New Mexico) because he had been one of the Woodcraft League boys. Maurice, a student of poetry

Top: Boy campers in Indian costume on the roof of the kiva at Seton Village, 1930s. Library and Archives Canada.

Middle: Hogan interior. Jack Hokeah, a member of the "Kiowa Five" artists, painted the interior murals in the 1930s. The murals were destroyed in subsequent years by water damage. Library and Archives Canada.

Bottom: Seton's library, ca. 1950s. Library and Archives Canada.

Right: Seton with Princess Chinquilla, daughter of a Cheyenne chief, at the College of Indian Wisdom, 1931.

Far right: Julia Seton in Woodcraft costume, 1930s. Photo Archives/Palace of the Governors.

Below: Julia Seton lecture promotional brochure, 1940s. Academy for the Love of Learning.

A New Series of Lectures

by MRS. ERNEST THOMPSON SETON

and philosophy, and Marceil, an artist, had purchased a printing press and wanted to create handmade books. Maurice later recalled that with Julia's "quick perception of mutual interests and possibilities, we were, within the hour, talking of moving our press to Seton Village." They set up shop in January 1938 and brought out twenty-four titles over the next four years, including a total of six written by either Seton or Julia. They hand-set the type for many of the books they printed—a page at a time—in an exercise in the finest artistic craftsmanship. Their masterpiece was the leather-bound essay by Seton, "The Buffalo Wind," the most sought-after Seton title today.

Seton's personal life took some dramatic turns during the 1930s. He finally became a U.S. citizen near the end of 1931, thirty-five years after first becoming a permanent resident. The end of another long-standing saga came when his long-hoped-for marriage to Julia finally took place. (Julia and Ted were divorced in the latter part of 1934, and Seton's divorce from Grace was granted on January 18, 1935. He and Julia married four days later in El Paso.) Their winter sojourn was soon interrupted, however, when Seton was hospitalized for a month due to prostate surgery. While he was in the hospital, he received two letters from Dan Beard, who renewed their acquaintance in a friendly way. Uncle Dan had mellowed over time, and, to some extent, so had Seton, who thanked Beard for thinking of him. (Beard and Baden-Powell had been similarly afflicted.) This began a correspondence that continued over the next six years, ending just a few months before Beard's death in June 1941. The two men groused about James West and tried to jog one another's memory about earlier days, becoming Scouting's version of Thomas Jefferson and John Adams, old enemies who found that their common experience outweighed the bitterness of past battles. Even so, given Beard's rancor toward him between 1910 and 1915, Seton must have been amazed at his new attitude:

> *In regard to the formation of Scouting, I only know the things in which I personally took part. Outside of that I leave to the other fellows who took part in it themselves, but I would like to see a real, unbiased history of the evolution and growth of the Movement itself, written by an outside party. Such a history is bound to be written sooner or later, by someone who will not be influenced by the personal claims of Ernest Thompson, Baden-Powell or Dan Beard. This will probably be done when you and I have the grass growing over our coverlid, and when we cannot make much of a kick, so why worry? All three of us have fought our fight, and we have fought a good fight, and the three of us have left our marks. And all three of us have now reached the point where years have mellowed our characters. We can now smile at things that used to irritate us, and now laugh at things that used to make us angry. We should be able to join in the old song: "So let the wide world way as it will, I will be gay and happy still."*
>
> *God bless you, old man, and good luck to you!*

Around this time, Seton was revising, as part of his autobiography, an unforgiving version about the origins of Scouting, which he ultimately decided not to publish. He kept the negative tone of his reminiscences out of his letters to Beard. One of his responses to Beard included birthday wishes for 1935.

> *Well, well, you are 87 and all's well. I remember the time when I used to think 70 a very old man. I don't now, as I am 77 [sic] myself and going strong. Our friendship began over 50 years ago and continues yet. Accept my congratulations on your life of usefulness. The boys of America have always loved you; now after these four score years, you are, I think, higher in public esteem than ever before.*

Even more remarkable than his renewed contact with Beard was a decision Seton and Julia made at the end of 1937, when they entered into an arrangement with an El Paso, Texas, family to adopt three young sisters. The circumstances that set this in motion are not known. The girls spent around two weeks over Christmas at Seton

Beulah "Dee" Seton
attends her first ceremony,
Seton Village, August 14,
1938. Library and Archives
Canada.

Castle, but when the Setons refused a condition of the adoption to raise the children as Catholics, the plan fell apart, and they drove the girls back to Texas. On their way back from El Paso in early February they stopped at Hot Springs, New Mexico, where Seton gave a talk at the just-opened Carrie Tingley Hospital for children. There they met (or learned of) a young pregnant woman from a nearby community who needed to give up her baby for adoption. Immediately upon their return to Seton Village, they designed a nursery attached to Julia's bedroom. The mother-to-be moved into Seton Castle by early April, and gave birth at a Santa Fe hospital on June 6, 1938. (She apparently left Santa Fe shortly afterward.) The *New Mexican* reported Seton's anticipation of once again becoming a father. Somewhat confusingly, the article was published five days after the birth of the child, who had been named Beulah. Making everything more muddled, the paper reported that Mrs. Seton had been taken to the hospital to await the birth of the child, her "first." Two days later, the paper printed Julia's denial that she was the mother, but it still didn't mention that the child had already been born. The paper's editors reported that Seton himself had provided the information they printed. It might have ended there, but by November, in an interview for the *New York World-Telegram*, Seton again suggested that he was the father. The interview seemed to have been done jointly with Julia; she didn't claim or disclaim being the mother, but did add that the new baby "looks just like her father. She has his black eyes and curly hair." She had inadvertently suggested that Seton had fathered the child with another woman, although there is no evidence that this actually could have been the case. Not knowing when to leave a subject alone, Julia also mentioned, "We would have preferred a son." For a couple used to dealing with the press and publicity, their handling of the announcement of little Beulah's arrival was nothing short of a debacle.

Within a few months, Beulah accompanied her parents on lecture tours, and by age three she appeared onstage with them performing Indian dances. (Some years after Seton's death, Beulah followed the family tradition by changing her first name to Dee. As Dee Seton Barber, she lived at Seton Village for much of her life. In 1968, when Julia moved to a new nearby house, Dee and her husband, Dale Barber, took up residence in Seton Castle, where they raised their two children. Julia died on April 29, 1975. Dee and Dale remained in Seton Castle until 1998, when Dee's respiratory condition forced them to move to a lower elevation; five years later they sold the Castle to the Academy for the Love of Learning. Dee died in Tennessee in 2006.)

Trailing Arbutus

By the beginning of World War II, Seton still maintained a high energy level, traveling constantly on lecture tours and finally making a little less work for himself by discontinuing the summer programs of the Seton Institute after 1940. The problems of maintaining Seton Village, however, proved overwhelming. In August, during the final session of the institute and just a day after his eightieth birthday, all the institute's staff quit, and renters of the village houses pulled out as well. Julia had almost cancelled the summer sessions earlier in the year; by August she probably wished she had followed through on that inclination. The reason for the disintegration of their program is not certain, but the fact that the staff all quit at the same time suggests that the institute could not meet its payroll. The problems only got worse as the war continued—renters skipped out before paying, and keeping or even finding employees to help maintain the property proved almost impossible. By mid-1943 they had entirely run out of money, and at last Seton began to feel his age, suffering from a number of minor ailments, none of which incapacitated him, but, taken together, forced him to slow down. Entries in his journal became less frequent and his always-terrible handwriting became noticeably weaker and even more difficult to read.

Julia and Ernest enjoy a light moment at the Castle, ca. 1940. Library and Archives Canada.

In his last years, Seton befriended Manly Hall, the young philosopher and founder of the Philosophical Research Society in Los Angeles. While Seton's other publishers had abandoned him, Hall helped with the editing and arranged for the printing of Seton's last book, *Santana, the Hero Dog of France.* They saw one another infrequently, and, with Seton's failing handwriting, kept touch by way of letters exchanged between Julia and Hall. The details of their friendship have not been recorded, but clearly the two men became close. During the summer of 1946, Hall began receiving letters from Julia in which she expressed her alarm at "the Chief's"

Induction of dogs into the Army, QM Depot
Front Royal, Va. August 25, 1942
"Brinker", a Great Pyrenees, on left and
"Kim", a Black Newfoundland on right.

Seton gathered this image of Brinker and Kim from the Army Signal Corps during the writing of his last, never-published 1943 book, *Animals in War.* Library and Archives Canada.

rapidly declining health. Seton nonetheless managed to deliver a final lecture at the University of New Mexico on his birthday, August 14. No record of the talk has turned up. Maybe he mentioned Lobo one last time in his final public appearance. In September, *Reader's Digest* ran an article on Seton entitled "Wild Animals He Has Known," concluding that Seton "will be remembered for leading millions of Americans to regard the creatures of the wilds as friends who bear the same touch of intangible greatness—and weakness—which distinguishes all thinking life." That month he was hospitalized, suffering from cancer of the pancreas (a condition only discovered with the autopsy). Doctors sent him home to the Castle to die, there being nothing else to do. Seton recorded his return from the hospital on September 6. He died on the morning of October 23. Afterward, Hall wrote to Julia.

Since your telephone call telling me of the Chief's passing, I have tried several times to write you but the words just wouldn't come. I was strangely drawn to the Chief from the first time I ever saw him, and although I knew him only a few years it seemed that I had known him all my life. Perhaps the fact that I have no memory of my own father, and always wanted to know him, has something to do with my feelings. I did not realize that I was an especially sentimental person, but the Chief's death has affected me more than anything else that has ever happened to me. So please forgive me, dear friend, if I have been silent these last few days—I just can't talk about it yet.

On Thursday evening I paid a simple tribute to the Chief at my lecture. I couldn't say much, but I know that our people knew that I spoke directly from my heart when I told them that the world had lost a great man and I had lost a very dear friend.

The Woodcrafters had often heard Seton recite (or chant) what he called the Omaha Tribal Prayer at the closing of their ceremonies. At Seton's memorial service on October 25, Stephen M. Jessup, one of the remaining Woodcrafters, recalled the words and used them at the end of their "council." He recited the prayer in English, and then in Omaha as he had heard it from Seton.

Father a needy one stands before thee;
I that sing am he.

Death and Transfiguration

Seton received a level of recognition in death that had eluded him in life. Tributes appeared in newspapers, magazines, and journals across the United States, emphasizing his influence in the conservation movement, Woodcraft, and literature. He would have been especially pleased at the validation of his work that appeared in a number of newspapers, including the *New York Times:* "His Birchbark Roll of the Woodcraft Indians originated the spirit of the Boy Scout movement in the United States."

Time magazine published an especially moving tribute:

> *One autumn day last week in Seton Village, N. Mex., death came to a man who, in an age of sweeping mechanization, had loved the natural earth, its seasons and its creatures, with rare intensity and an unusual power to communicate his vision to others. To three generations of children whom his stories of wild life had introduced to the life of woods and fields, to naturalists indebted to the scope and minute fidelity of his discernments, Ernest Thompson Seton's death was something like the falling of a forest tree.*

In his final years, Seton often wrote about the "money-madness" that he saw as the cause of many of the world's ills. He wrote in *The Gospel of the Redman*, "The civilization of the Whiteman is a failure; it is visibly crumbling around us. It has failed at every crucial test. No one who measures things by results can question this fundamental statement." He felt that greed as practiced by Western civilization was a vice mostly unknown to the traditional tribal peoples of North

Top: Seton and Gray Whirlwind speak through sign language, ca. 1920s. Seton published a book on the subject, *Sign Talk*, in 1918. SIRIS/Smithsonian.

Bottom: Seton at prayer, probably at the Castle, 1940s. Library and Archives Canada.

America. This was a remarkable statement for the time, implying a superiority of the "Redman" over whites. It also defined greed as a cultural attribute, not as a biological or inherent one. That is to say, while white Western culture is more or less stuck with its genetic inheritance, Seton believed its cultural habits can be changed—indeed, *must* be changed—in order to avoid "Divine vengeance and total destruction." Seton noted that, in traditional Native American society, an individual's status was measured by how much he or she served the larger community, not by how much wealth was acquired. For him, the pan-Indian culture epitomized how to live a non-dogmatic, democratic, egalitarian life.

"Stone Man." A photograph of an Indian man, probably taken by Seton, n.d. Library and Archives Canada.

Seton's criticism of white culture extended to contemporary issues of native rights. He was, like other New Mexico artists, a supporter of John Collier, Commissioner of Indian Affairs in the Franklin D. Roosevelt administration. Collier, unlike earlier commissioners, was an advocate for native sovereignty and a supporter of native cultural values. He and Seton shared outrage over the continuing violation of Indian treaty rights, made worse because native peoples had almost no legal rights in U.S. courts. Seton had intended the Red Lodge of the Woodcraft League to address these issues. He proposed extending citizenship to American Indians, closing the boarding schools Indian children were forced to attend, and restoring lands stolen in violation of treaty rights. "By repeated making and breaking of successive treaties," he wrote, "the whites at length arbitrarily acquired the whole country. We realize today that this was done by fraud and massacre."

In his late writing, Seton also explored many of the life events that had had a deep emotional impact on him. These were spontaneous mystical experiences, some associated with wild nature, others occurring in more ordinary circumstances. On his first trip to Manitoba he was nearly killed when he stepped off the back of a moving train, catching onto a railing at the last possible instant. Later, his mother told him, "God surely has work for you to do." In *Trail of an Artist-Naturalist*, he compared his early, deeply felt awakening to the awesome experience of wilderness to living in a "dream world." He recalled: "From my earliest years I longed to be a naturalist. I thought I had a mission—to be the prophet of outdoor life." On the prairies of Manitoba, he was transfixed by the song of a thrasher: "Spiritually, I kneeled before him . . . He had me full possessed . . . my very soul seemed but the organ on which the singer king had played." While on a hunting trip, he nearly drowned in a bog, tangled in mud and roots, helplessly sinking. Then, suddenly, his feet struck hard ground, and he sank no more. (Apparently a real event, but also a metaphor for a spiritual storm and its resolution.) "When alone in these silent places," he wrote, "I felt surging through me so strong a gush of glorious exhilaration that no trouble in my mind could stand before it."

But it was in "The Buffalo Wind" essay of 1938 where Seton became most revelatory, influenced by his immersion in the study of Indian wisdom. The Buffalo Wind, he explained, was a guiding force that motivated his movements across continents. The sound of wind had been responsible for the experience of spontaneous epiphanies, sometimes sending him into a trancelike state. As a small child, he heard the wind in an Aeolian harp and was gripped by a "sweet agony" that reached his "inmost being." As a boy, he heard it in the trees at Glenyan: "I flung myself on the ground, and bit the twigs in a craze of longing and inexpression." As an art student in London, the extreme asceticism he practiced led him into a state of "dreaming dreams": "I began to hear the Voices. I heard them in the ecstatic time that comes near sunrise, when my body seemed to float in the peace that passeth all understanding." He experienced the opposite while reading about a nineteenth-century atrocity in California: "the Indians of Shasta were massacred—massacred by the Christians—all their love and dreams of the Great Mountain were forgotten. . . . There was no human sound—the quail whistled in the grass, and the wind moaned in the cedars and the grass, and moaned farewell. My eyes blurred . . . The book dropped from my hand for, 'The Buffalo Wind was blowing!'" And as an art student in Paris, it came to him in his sleep: "a song that clutched and wracked me—a thrilling song that hurt me more than I can ever tell." He concluded this remarkable account with three cryptic sentences.

> *The swift years have gone—the urge becomes a lash. I am going now—I am going with all my strength. So have I sought a homeland under the white Snow Peaks—where Trail meets Trail—and far away, flashing and bright, the Red Man's River seeks the open sea.*

"The Buffalo Wind" begins with Seton's outcry as a small child: "I want to go! I want to go!" To where, he has no idea, but he seems bound for a special destination in life's journey. The essay concludes: "I am going now." These are the places of his internal landscape; the homeland is the homeland of the soul, wherever that may be. The river seeking the sea is like the individual soul merging with the larger cosmos at death. Seton's wording is purposely vague, for as a believer in natural religion, he does not accept anyone else's religious revelation as valid for him, and neither does he invite us along with him—this revelation is purely personal. He does, however, have a purpose in the sharing: he suggests that the way also exists for us if we have the fortitude to seek it.

Seton at play with a wolf, 1930s. Library and Archives Canada.

The transformative experience symbolized by the Buffalo Wind is essentially ecological in nature: everything is in motion, everything recycles to become something else, everything is in wild unison like the *ollins*, the symbols of change that whirl through Seton's drawings. His own chaotic leanings were a contradictory whirl—romantic naturalist and Cartesian scientist, academic illustrator and synoptic cartoonist, preservationist and hunter—but these aspects of Seton were also his attempt to reach an integral life, with the pursuit of knowledge at the core of everything. Seton attached

The last formal portrait of
Seton, probably taken in
Los Angeles at a Woodcraft
League meeting, 1946.
Library and Archives
Canada.

two symbols to represent this process, the buffalo horn emblem of Woodcraft and the wolf paw print drawn under his signature—wisdom and perseverance met with courage and integrity. The buffalo and the wolf appear to be enemies, but on the ecological level, they are essential to each other's well-being, complementary aspects of a larger whole. This reconciliation of opposites is the higher purpose, the mystical meaning, of Woodcraft.

New Mexico provided Ernest Thompson Seton with the environment he required for deep spiritual reflection, first in the winter of 1893, and then again in the 1930s and up to the end of his life. Ever present in that process was his keenly felt responsibility for causing the death of Lobo. The King of Currumpaw, specimen #677, a seventy-eight-pound male gray wolf of the semi-arid grasslands, had, in his way, worked a kind of magic. By forcing Seton to ask "WHY?" Lobo helped him on his journey from wolf killer to student of the Buffalo Wind. Seton made a transformation within himself, putting the best of what he had learned to work its way in the world—where it is working still.

Acknowledgments

BULL BUFFALO IN NATIONAL MUSEUM GROUP.
Drawn by Ernest E. Thompson.

My professional home of the last several years has been with the Academy for the Love of Learning in Santa Fe, New Mexico. I began work with their Seton art collection in 2004, soon after it was acquired from Dee Seton Barber. This has been the opportunity of a lifetime. My deepest gratitude goes to Academy founder and president Aaron Stern.

The Philmont Ranch, Boy Scouts of America, has been vital. Philmont Museum director Seth McFarland was essential to the development of the exhibition and in his support for this book. I began my Seton studies at Philmont in 1972 when Kent Bush was director, followed by the incomparable Ellie Pratt.

The New Mexico History Museum has allowed me to present some of my Seton findings in a major exhibition. Director Frances Levine, PhD, supported the idea from the first day I presented it to her.

Gibbs Smith, the publisher of this book, believed in the project from the start, and worked with me to get it going in the right direction. My editor, Jared Smith, has brought the focus and clarity needed to this complex subject.

I never met Dee Seton Barber, but I would like to acknowledge that she and her family (and a few highly motivated friends) devoted untold hours over many decades working at keeping the Seton legacy alive. Her presence has been part of this project.

Seton's granddaughter Pamela Forcey was one of two main outside readers of the manuscript. She brought editorial skills and knowledge of family history. My other reader, Robert G. Hare, has worked with me in close collaboration on literary, artistic, and wilderness ventures for almost forty years since we discovered Seton together at Philmont.

My longtime Taos friend—and exceptional artist—Marsha Skinner has engaged me in esoteric and intellectual conversations for this project, and others, leading to ideas I would not have thought of on my own.

Special thanks to my favorite naturalist, David Attenborough.

I received important help from Seton descendants: Dr. Clemency Chase Coggins (granddaughter), Crista Coggins Franklin (great-granddaughter), Julie Seton (granddaughter), Dale Barber (son-in-law), and David Thompson (great-grand-nephew) and his wife, Eleanor May.

In Cimarron, New Mexico: former Philmont general manager Keith Gallaway, former museum director Jason Schubert, librarian Robin Taylor, and advisors Amy Flowers and Dave Emery.

At the Academy for the Love of Learning in Santa Fe: Vivi Pollock, David Gordon, Eleanor Makris, Donato Jaggers, Marianne Murray, Dan Brannen, Sage Magdalene, Anna Sanchez, Mark Nicolson, Reta Lawler, Melissa Stevens-Briceno, Tina Olson, Matthew Fox, Crissie Orr, Robin Weeks, Patty Nagle, Philip Snyder, Drew Nucci, and others who have crossed my path more briefly. The Academy for the Love of Learning provides a range of programming in education and leadership, with information available at www.aloveoflearning.org.

Several researchers were most important in helping me understand Seton: John H. Wadland, PhD, Lucinda MacKethan, PhD, David L. Braddell, Bill Taylor, John G. Samson, and Ronald L. Edmonds.

Santa Fe and Albuquerque advisors: Lucy Moore, Barbara Witemeyer, Jerry Zollars, Kim Straus (Brindle Foundation), and Dieter Rall.

Television producer Brian Leith and director Steve Gooder. Their production for BBC/PBS, *Lobo, The Wolf That Changed America*, allowed me to try out important ideas about Seton and Lobo.

At the New Mexico History Museum (including the Palace of the Governors, the oldest public building in America): Louise Stiver, René Harris, Caroline Lajoie, Natalie Baca, Erica García, Daniel Kosharek, and Tom Leech.

Also, Patricia Loughridge, Ellen Firsching Brown, Elizabeth Lane Coulter, Anne Young (The Historical Society, Town of Greenwich, Connecticut), and the staff of Library and Archives Canada in Ottawa. And to anyone else not mentioned above who should have received credit here.

And to the art history dogs, labs Lucca and Lucia, and Lobo (red rough collie).

And to my partner in life (and in the adjoining office), Bonnie Schermerhorn.

Appendixes

Appendix 1
Extended Note On Ancestry

In 1899 Monsignor Robert Seton published his monumental forty-year study, *An Old Family, Or, The Setons of Scotland and America.* Both Ernest Thompson Seton (ETS) and his daughter Ann (Anya Seton) read the book, probably avidly, as the family owned three copies, all of which include annotations in various hands. One has ETS's signature inside the front cover. ETS used this source to help document his identity as a Seton, especially as a "direct descendant," as he claimed, of an earlier George Seton, the fifth Earl of Winton, who lost the family titles and lands in the 1715 Jacobite uprising. According to ETS in his autobiography, Winton's only lawful heir was a George Seton of Bellingham in Northumberland, first cousin to ETS's father, Joseph Logan Thompson:

> *In 1823, after the general amnesty* [of Jacobites, which had taken place in 1747], *this George Seton appeared before the Bailies of Cannongate, the highest tribunal in Scotland; and proved himself the only grandson and lawful heir of George Seton, Earl of Winton. The bailies* [Scottish aldermen] *acknowledged the validity of the claim, and George Seton was served with the title of Earl of Winton. He died without issue, but named my father as his heir and the lawful successor to the title, as he was the only male survivor of the line. My father's grandmother was Ann Seton. She never ceased to urge our people to make a stand for their rights. My father always meant to do so; but his natural indolence effectually stopped all action. On her deathbed, his grandmother, in these, her last words, enjoined him: "Never forget, Joseph, you are the heir. You are Seton, the Earl of Winton. You must stand up for your rights."*

This is a wonderful story—except that its primary conclusion about the existence of the Winton/Seton title is demonstrably false. ETS must have known from Monsignor Seton and other peerage records that the Lord Seton and Earl of Winton titles were extinct. (A Winton title was re-created in the 1800s, but that is the story of another family.) ETS's quoted statement by Grandmother Ann to Joseph also was not correct. His misstatement could have happened because he no longer had Joseph's letter to George Seton (ETS's brother) recounting possible connections to the earlier George Seton (his mother's cousin and Winton's grandson) and was recalling it to memory decades later. Joseph's version in his letter to George was that his grandmother Ann spoke these final words to his mother (whose name was Mary): "Now, Mary, mind, Joseph's the heir." Joseph didn't say whether or not he actually heard those words, and neither did he claim to be the heir to anything; he was just reporting what he recalled from decades earlier. More to the point, Joseph identified himself as a Cameron, not as a Seton. So why would ETS claim the title of Winton for his father when it clearly no longer existed, and, even if it had, interested his father not at all? ETS had been in full rebellion against his father for as long as either of them could remember—he nearly admitted something close to hatred for the man. Since Joseph thought of himself as a Cameron, perhaps it was to be expected that ETS would identify himself as a Seton just to accentuate the differences between the two, as if such were needed. His father did not approve of ETS taking the Seton name, and ETS himself did not use it publicly until after his mother's death. One other of Joseph's sons, George, also took the name Seton, while another took Cameron; the others appear to have remained Thompsons. Joseph's ancestral family had the name Cameron until 1745, when, in another unsuccessful Stuart attempt to regain the English and Scottish thrones, Joseph's great-great-grandfather, Evan (or Alan) Cameron, supported the "Young Pretender," Charles Edward Stuart ("Bonnie Prince Charlie"). After that rebellion fell apart, Evan fled from English reprisals in Scotland by moving to England, just across the border, hiding under the assumed name Thompson, which as a name suited Joseph just fine. In 1745, Evan managed to accomplish just what the fifth Earl of Winton had achieved in 1715, namely, losing all the family fortune. By chance, ETS's mother's family, the Biddlestones, had lost everything in that same 1745 rebellion. Thus had the Seton-Wintons, Camerons, and Biddlestones handed down to their descendants an across-the-board legacy of total, absolute defeat: no property, no titles. But they left something else—a record of undaunted courage and fidelity to Scotland that was the source of great pride to their descendants. ETS could have claimed all these ancestors equally, but he chose to emphasize the Seton part of his legacy. While the Seton and Winton titles were extinct, ETS's claim to be a Seton had validity, even if the connection was rather indirect.

The name "Seton" has no special resonance in America, but in Scotland, the Setons were leading patriots who fought the English through generations until their final defeat in 1715. There are no families in the United States or Canada quite like the Setons of Scotland. ETS knew this, and his name change reflects his relationship with both celebrity and personal identity. He loved celebrity—loved being one himself and keeping company with others so-called. To know ETS we must know the Setons who were (according to the monsignor) at various times Scots, Normans, and Norse. ETS took as his heroic ideal the American Indian rather than Vikings or Scots, in part at least because he knew them in person rather than from

history books. Scottish heroism, however, is not unlike that of North America's natives, with personal valor and great integrity as common traits. History is, of course, messier than this simplification, but the Scots' saga gave Ernest Evan Thompson the impetus to become Ernest Thompson Seton.

According to our guide into this saga, Robert Seton,

> *The Setons are essentially a Scottish family, and, like all the historical families of Scotland, are of Norman origin. It is, moreover, one of the few families in Great Britain that can be traced back to Normandy, and was found established there before the Conquest of England; consequently it is one of the oldest families in Europe . . . nearly all the Norman nobility* [were] *. . . descended from the Royal House of Norway.*

The origin of Scottish families is vastly more complicated than Robert Seton indicated, but here we will look at family history the way ETS understood it. ETS's concern in any event was with the post-Conquest family. Whatever their origin, the Setons emerge from the mists of time after the fall of the Roman Empire, where facts and myths often collide.

The principal "baronial families" appeared in the eleventh century. The Normans established (or re-established or co-established) the use of surnames; in any event, they introduced this convention to Britain after the Conquest. Never underestimate the pride of name once established or the lengths to which that pride may be defended. Names connote heredity and territory—commodities tradable by marriage and to be won or lost in conquest. A name associated with one of history's winners, such as William the Conqueror, is to be particularly cherished. But the Setons, the monsignor tells us, go back even before William took England and Scotland for his prize. The Normans (no doubt accompanied by knights from other nationalities) took over in a manner so absolute as to defy anything in our contemporary experience, wiping out much of the existing

tribal gentry. William, orphaned at age seven, survived his boyhood in the treacherous medieval world long enough to take part on the winning side in a 1047 cavalry battle that confirmed him as the Duke of Normandy. His career was basically on an upward trend from then on, including making an alliance with Flanders, benefiting from an invasion of England by Norwegians, and taking advantage of the appearance of Halley's Comet in 1066 (a good omen for William). It was all too much for England's King Harold, whose Saxons went down fighting, and went down hard. William, to complete his work, did so by becoming one of the most infamous mass murderers of his time; perhaps, in terms of percentage of the population killed, one of the most infamous of any time. The Scots held out longer than the Saxons, but they largely gave in to William in 1072, marking the beginning of a new chapter in centuries of unpleasantness with their neighbors to the south.

Robert Seton claims the Picts of Say (a town in Normandy) as the ancestral Setons and says that some of them must have accompanied William on his tour of England. The lineage was ancient, traced back before 1000 AD. The first to live in eleventh-century Scotland was Saire de Say (one of many spellings), named for a hermit-saint popular with the Normans; his son was Du-gall de Say-toun, "du-gall" being a Scots term for "black stranger," applied by Picts and others to the Normans in their armor. The surname had turned into de Setoune by 1179. ("De Say" could change because people of that time sometimes took as their names the geographic name of their location. Those of Say could add the suffix "ton," or of "the lord"; or "tun," meaning the "dwelling of.") The family headquarters was built near Edinburgh. Into the 1200s, the de Setounes were not yet Scots but were feudal lords who spoke Norman and/or French, marrying into the families of other continental invaders for decade after decade. Their rule was ruthless—only through violence (or threat thereof) could they lord over the rustic population they had conquered. They were

granted the right by the Conqueror's son Henry I and his successors to control markets (that is, profit from the economic system) and to execute criminals—male wrongdoers by hanging and females by the more genteel drowning in wells. During the first decade of the 1200s, Adam de Setoune broke the usual pattern of being solely concerned with murder, rapine, and hunting. He is noted in the family history as something of a scholar; literacy, even among the nobility, was somewhat exceptional in those times. His son Chrystell has his name entered into the records as "de Seton." (The French-Norman speakers used the "de" prefix.) When that language died out of regular use in Scotland, the "de" died with it. Chrystell continued his father's habit of reading and is said to have added prayer to his repertoire as well. But it was his son, probably born before the mid-1200s, Sir Christopher Seton, who may be the one who made the transition from Norman to Scot.

This Seton started one long and tragic family tradition of warring against the English, and another, related, of being in the company of the most famous Scots, including the biggest celebrity Scot of all, Sir William Wallace. Everyone wants to own a piece of someone this big, so the facts of his life are of course in dispute. He likely was not the semi-peasant savage of the movie *Braveheart*. Like George Washington, he was a landowner with a lot to lose through the wrong kind of change. He was, however, also a Scots patriot. That the national hero of Scotland had Christopher Seton II as his companion in the terrible struggle for power between the kings John Balliol and Robert Bruce (and various others) was not lost on ETS. King Edward I ("Longshanks") of England conquered Wales and also interfered with Scotland by supporting various sides in their wars by both political intrigue and direct military intervention. Edward got rid of John Balliol (King John I). Robert Bruce (King Robert I) worked both for and against Edward. William Wallace (apparently more a supporter of Balliol than of Bruce) was there to clean up the mess

–Distant views and characteristic outlines of :
Gray-wolf,
Coyote,
Fox.

left by the royals—with Christopher Seton by his side. Wallace may have been of Celtic ancestry, and like Christopher probably had some education. Recall that Christopher was of Norman (or Flemish) ancestry. It appears that differences in origin were beginning to be submerged into Scottishness, which could be leveraged into working together against a common enemy. The record (as put forward by the monsignor) is mute as to whether Christopher took part in Wallace's great victory at Stirling Bridge or the lesser ones elsewhere, although he almost certainly would have been present for at least some, if not all of them. He might have died with so many others at the Falkirk disaster in July 1298 had he not met his end in another battle with the English a month earlier. No longer Norman or Flemish or whatever, Christopher was a true Scots martyr. And he was a Seton. To ETS, English by birth, Canadian by nationality, American by adoption, but Scots by ancestry, Christopher's sacrifice would have been meaningful.

For the next four and a half centuries, whenever Scotland needed champions in her defense, Setons frequently took to the front lines. The United States has not yet been around long enough to build this kind of heritage. But let us for a moment create a fantasy league starting with General Nathanael Greene, one of the few able and accomplished generals of the American War of Independence. And then let us imagine that his sons and grandsons (or granddaughters) took leading, occasionally even central, roles in the War of 1812, the Mexican War, the Civil War, the Spanish-American War, and so on until the conflict in Iraq and, in addition, in all the other wars in which America may be involved for the next two hundred years. The first General Greene would be honored (rather than forgotten) as scion of a hero family of the nation. This example gives some idea of the place held in Scotland (at least at the suggestion of Robert Seton and doubtless in the mind of ETS) by the warrior Setons. To be associated with them is to be associated with greatness, a most important association

in the psychology of certain persons. It also sets a very, very high standard. Whoever tries to really change the world, even a little, has made a commitment of a high order, one that probably involves some kind of sacrifice along the way. ETS seems to have left little record of what direct impact Christopher and that knight's successors had on his own life. But he was aware of them, and, by taking the name of Seton, he was consciously aligning himself with their legacy, doing so in a way that the names Thompson, Snowdon, Biddlestone, or even Cameron could not.

Had the Seton family story peaked with Wallace, they could still have made some claim on the legend, but with Christopher, it was just beginning. Christopher III won knighthood a few years later for his service to King Robert Bruce. He became "Seton of Seton," that is, (Lord) Seton of the (place) Seton, an honor of the highest order. (That centuries later, ETS would build his own "Seton Village" in New Mexico, thus himself becoming at a later time Seton of Seton, is a direct reflection of Bruce's accolade to Christopher Seton III.) Bruce himself was nearly killed in the 1306 battle at Methven (near Perth), but was saved by Christopher III (who had become Bruce's brother-in-law five years before by marriage to the king's sister). Monsignor Robert Seton recites an old story that Bruce was almost betrayed by the duplicitous Scots knight, Sir Philip de Mowbray, whom Christopher killed with a broadsword kept for all subsequent time by the family in Edinburgh. But, like ETS's story of his father's unclaimed title, this one too is false. Mowbray continued to take a role in local politics for many years after Methven, working on Bruce's behalf. More clear is that Christopher III gained his chance to become a martyr when he actually was betrayed to the English. Interestingly, a memorial chapel built for this warrior at Berwick-on-Tweed was cannibalized for the fortifications of the town during the Jacobite insurgency of 1715, which so greatly influenced the subsequent fortunes—or misfortunes—of the Seton family. Although his memorial was destroyed, it should have pleased Christopher to know its loss helped to inflict additional pain on the English.

It is simply unavoidable to mention one more battle. While Setons seemed to come and go, King Robert Bruce remained, surviving long enough to be served by yet another of the clan, Alexander, who also played an important role in the massive English defeat at Bannockburn in 1314. There the Scots used a military formation known as a *schiltrom*, a tightly packed group of "spearmen" (Winston Churchill's term) whose earlier antecedent was the phalanx evolved by Philip II of Macedon. Said to have been developed by William Wallace (who had been executed by the English in 1305), the schiltrom featured a group of men who moved with outward-facing pikes that could be implanted in the ground to entirely defeat oncoming cavalry. This human porcupine formation was fearsome up close but just as vulnerable to being shot as our strange little quilled mammals. The schiltrom was defenseless against the English longbow, which could easily decimate the conveniently compacted soldiers. Knowing this, Bruce was loath to attack the English, who had regrettably shown up in superior numbers. Bruce's young retainer Alexander Seton convinced Bruce that a surprise attack in schiltrom formation would catch the English with their archers down. And it worked—scores of English noble knights were slaughtered. The English king, Edward II, retreated to Stirling Castle, where (according to Robert Seton) the supposedly dead Philip de Mowbray was in residence. Like other Scots (including Bruce), Mowbray at various times supported either England or Scotland. In this case he kept his doors locked to the defeated Edward. If Mowbray wasn't dead, he was expedient. Three hundred years later, poet Patrick Gordon would write:

Three thousand more came forth of Lothian fair.
All Princes, Lords, and Knights, and men of Fame,
Where Seton's Lord, e'en Winton's Earl, did bear

Not meanest Rule, with others of great Name.

Actually, the Setons would not get the Winton title for a while yet. Typically, Alexander Seton couldn't get enough of fighting the English and was finally killed by them in 1332 during the dreary, endless struggle between the two nations, in which so many Setons died that it is surprising enough were around to reproduce.

But so they did, through the fourth Alexander. He, however, missed the genetic boat by going to his reward (not in battle) before fathering a son. And this is where the Seton story takes an interesting turn. Alexander's only daughter, Margaret, was "abducted" by a neighbor, Baron Alan de Winton, in 1347. The kidnapper was caught and the aggrieved Margaret was herself allowed to choose whatever punishment she wished to mete out against de Winton. How he must have squirmed at the thought of what might lie ahead. Ah, the cruelty of women! She chose to have him marry her, and they were, according to the chronicles, "happy ever afterward." Lord de Winton must have been especially happy to have escaped being drawn and quartered for rape, and, in a rare case of eating your cake and having it too, he also gained control of the vast Seton properties. Indeed, while still possibly breathing a sigh of relief over the outcome, he changed his surname to Seton, while retaining his title and passing on to his de Winton sons the title Lord Seton.

Over the next couple of centuries there followed many more of this ilk (fighting the English and experiencing other adventures) known variously as "Lord Seton" or "Master of Seton." Around 1585, they added an additional title, Earl of Winton. There followed the second, third, and fourth Earls of Winton and the ill-fated fifth earl, named George. Following family tradition, he jumped at the chance to fight the English when he joined the Jacobite uprising in 1715 in support of the Catholic Stuart pretender to the throne, "James III," as he called himself (he was the

son of the deposed Catholic king, James II), who wanted to be king of both England and Scotland. The Protestant Stuarts had lost the throne to George I of the Protestant House of Hanover by inheritance in 1714. This time, the Roman Catholic Setons were in real trouble. The monsignor wrote about George: "He seems, like all his family, to have been given to study and researches of some kind, and to travel. . . . He was one of the first Scottish noblemen who played an active part in the 'Rising' of 1715, to restore the exiled family to the throne." Imagine this, a scholar who liked to travel and was not afraid of a fight.

For his part in this ill-fated war, after the fast-coming defeat in battle in Lancashire, George Seton joined others of his party who were lodged in the Tower of London for the next year or so. Being a Seton (that is, stubborn), he capitulated not one bit to King George. He was reputed to have made a punning joke about his executioner. His insolence may have been made easier by his having worked out an escape plan, or perhaps the joking was part of the plan to throw his jailers off the track. However that may be, he supposedly cut through the iron bars of his cell with a watch-spring and thereafter miraculously escaped. The watch-spring has not survived for inspection; perhaps he just bribed someone to let him out. He made his way to Rome, where he lived for many years. Eventually he died in Italy or back in Scotland or somewhere else, and with his passing came to an end the six-hundred-year Seton-Winton line of East Lothian. They said of this George Seton: "Lord Winton's character was very original, and he was calumniated by enemies and misunderstood by friends. . . ." This was also a trait of the later Seton.

George had a son who had a son who had a son, but none of them had much of a claim—all the titles had been extinguished in punishment (along with loss of all the property) for having supported the "Old Pretender," James III. The monsignor gave his version:

There have been claimants to the Winton peerage, but they have not succeeded. In 1825 a young man named George Seton [Joseph Logan Thompson's cousin George, or the uncle of his cousin, also named George] appeared at Edinburgh and called for the honors—the estates had been confiscated, sold, and dispersed; and although he probably was the grandson [or the great-grandson] of the fifth Earl of Winton [Joseph at least thought so], the want of a certificate of marriage between his grandfather and Margaret McKlear, daughter of a Scotch physician, settled his claim adversely.

ETS read this and yet published just the opposite conclusion to the inquiry. It is not even clear which George, a grandson or great-grandson, may have been the claimant. The story might have ended here, except that the fifth Earl of Winton had a granddaughter Ann—one wonders what happened to Winton's son—the very same Ann Seton Logan who told her daughter, Mary Ann Logan, that Mary's son, Joseph Logan Thompson (ETS's father), was the heir to the Winton title. The title that Joseph did not claim. The title that no longer existed.

Even if it had existed, the earldom was barren of assets. Both Joseph and his father, Enoch Thompson, being practical and thrifty Scots (even after having lived in England through three earlier generations as Camerons/Thompsons), apparently thought that gaining control of an empty Seton/Winton title was of no use to the Cameron clan. ETS had a different opinion, and, all things considered, such conflicts are exactly what make a good story. ETS did not believe that keeping all the facts exactly in order was the best way into a good story. A good story, as is known to any bard, is one that holds your attention, be it the exploits of warrior Scots or those of cattle-killing wolves.

So why did ETS claim the continuance of the non-existent Winton (and thus Seton) title? Apparently, he needed on a deep level to prove to himself a formal connection to the Seton mystique. No one else in America would have cared. So was this legitimacy of title-claim purposeful fabrication on his part? Perhaps not. Perhaps he had in his own mind transposed the unfair rejection in Edinburgh of the title into what actually should have occurred: its reasonable acceptance. But he need not have bothered, not for our sake. The Seton warrior traits of courage, personal honor, thirst for knowledge—traits he especially admired in the American Indian—all these were his as well. No title conferred by any king would have enhanced what was already present. Ernest Thompson Seton really was Seton of Seton.

Appendix 2
Early Figures in Conservation

The National Wildlife Federation, an environmental organization founded in 1937, created the "Conservation Hall of Fame" in the 1960s to honor Americans "who kept the wild alive in our world." Several of these "hall of famers" built reputations as both writers and naturalists, and may be credited as among the most important founders of the conservation movement. This short list is presented here to give additional historical context to the early conservation/environmental movement.

The work of Henry David Thoreau (1817–1862) influenced all the others. He combined natural history and transcendental philosophy to create the idea of what we would come to see as a conservation and environmental ethic. In 1851 he delivered a talk (later published as an essay) in which he put forward an idea that all subsequent environmentalists would take to heart: "The West of which I speak is but another name for the Wild; and what I have been preparing to say is, that in Wildness is the preservation of the World." Seton discovered his writing during his early studies in London.

John Burroughs (1837–1921) became the first widely read nature writer, helping to establish his field of study as a literary genre for the others who followed. He popularized the idea that holding regard for the sanctity of nature for its own sake was a valid intellectual

position. Seton also became acquainted with his work while in London and found in Burroughs a role model for becoming a writer and naturalist. The two later became friends, but not until after the old man did considerable damage to Seton by accusing him of being a "sham" naturalist. Burroughs was a close friend of Theodore Roosevelt.

John Muir (1838–1914) was the first environmentalist. In the early 1900s, two broad divisions—preservation and utilitarianism, represented by Muir and Gifford Pinchot respectively—defined conservation. Muir cofounded the Sierra Club and helped inspire the movement that resulted in a great expansion of national parks and monuments and the preservation of wilderness generally. His seminal work on the natural history of glaciers stands as an important scientific achievement. His literary works stand as among the most important in American literature. Among his great quotes: "When we try to pick out anything by itself, we find it hitched to everything else in the universe." He helped Theodore Roosevelt develop a conservation ethic. He was acquainted with both Burroughs and Seton, with whom he exchanged information about wildlife.

William Temple Hornaday (1854–1937) was, along with his close friend Seton, a founder of wildlife conservation. His efforts to save the American bison (through a conservation organization) were critical to its survival as a species. He founded the Camp Fire Club, an organization of outdoorsmen whose interests included wildlife preservation and the creation of national parks. Seton supported him in both of these efforts, including charter memberships in both organizations and serving as president of the Camp Fire Club from 1909 to 1910. Hornaday held senior positions at the Smithsonian and New York Zoological Park.

Theodore Roosevelt (1858–1919) greatly expanded the role of government in preserving our natural heritage through protection of wildlife and wild areas. He helped establish the foundations of the US Forest Service and enhanced the Biological Survey. He founded

the Boone and Crocket Club in 1887, which promoted scientific study and preservation of big-game animals (although largely for the purpose of hunting them) and promoted the creation of park and forest reserves. He urged Seton to produce *Lives of Northern Animals*, but he also had reservations about Seton's romantic notions of wildlife.

Appendix 3
Seton and Baden-Powell Correspondence

Ernest Thompson Seton and Robert S. S. Baden-Powell exchanged a series of letters important to understanding the youth outdoor-education movement, including the development of the Woodcraft League and the Boy Scouts. Seton kept a few dozen letters from the correspondence. They remained in the collection of the Seton family until they were gifted to the Library and Archives Canada in Ottawa, Ontario, where they constitute one part of the extensive Seton papers. Excerpts from a few of the letters follow below.

31 Oct. 06

Dear Seton

I enclose a kind of preliminary notice which I sent out early this year regarding my scheme of 'Boy Scouts'—and it has a very encouraging response—but I have to wait till this month before I can get under way with the details of it, though I have planned them. You will see that our principles seem practically identical, except that mine does not necessarily make its own organization— it is applicable to existing ones. If we can work together in the same direction I sh' be very glad indeed—for I'm sure that there are great possibilities before us.

I have ordered 'Aids to Scouting' to be sent to you.

November 3, 1906

My dear General,

Yours of the 31st October duly received, with the preliminary Paper on "Scouts," also "Aids to Scouting." I read both through with the greatest interest. I am not at all surprised that the "Aid" has run through so many editions. It is exactly the sort of thing that I am trying to carry on in America, though of course my experience has been very trifling, and I have added one or two features to the idea . . .

The Iron Hoofs [aka "tracking irons"] that I showed you I will send you . . . Later on I can send you a more scientifically made pair. Of course you understand these were made for use in Deer Hunting and also for the purpose of trailing . . .

I return herewith your manuscript about boy scouts. It certainly is admirable throughout as an idea, and cannot fail of wide acceptance throughout the country as well as in America.

10 Nov. 06

Dear Seton

I was very sorry to miss you—and am more sorry that I can say that all your dates for lectures just agree with the dates on which I am away from London . . .

I am studying one of your articles on tracks with great interest—and will return it . . . If you read my "Aids to Scouting" you will see somewhat similar ideas expressed— but not demonstrated by diagrams as yours is—and that is everything in teaching the young ideas.

17 June, 07

My Dear Seton

. . . I am now quietly working up my scheme for the Boy Scouts with most flattering encouragement from various authorities.

Notably Mr. Arthur Pearson, proprietor of Pearson's Magazine, Standard, Evening Standard, and other periodicals . . .

I have arranged next month to have a small camp of boys at which I propose to test the scheme before finally bringing out the book . . .

And any quotations I take from Birch Bark Roll I will acknowledge as such, and will copyright any wholesale extracts in your name.

I should indeed be proud to be connected as you suggest with your scouting branch—I only fear lest my delay to say so may have cut me out of it—but perhaps I may have sent you a line to say so. I hope I did . . .

Boy Scouts, Coschen Buildings, Henrietta Street, London, W. C.

24 Jan. 08

Dear Thompson Seton,

You will infer from the above address that we are going on with my scheme like your "Woodcraft Indians." And it promises well. I hope that you will allow me to make frequent mention of yourself and your tribes as examples to Scouts . . .

If you are going lecturing again in England let me know if I can be of any use with introductions to people at various places. And if you can in your lectures give a good word for the Boy Scouts scheme—it would, coming from you, be a most valuable help in spreading it.

13 Feb. 08

My dear Seton

Please forgive this scrawl written in the train. I wrote to you the other day in America telling you how I had been able to make a start with my scheme of Scouting for Boys much on the lines of your Woodcraft Indians— and sending you the Handbook, etc. But now

I hear you are in England and about to visit Wakefield where I was lecturing last night: so I send this in hope of catching you there.

Do tell me your moves. I should like so much to meet you again and have a chat and get you to meet some people who would interest you.

Also I want to know whether your tracking irons are *PATENT* [added in hand-printed letters in the typescript of the letter] *and may I have some made like them calling them the "Seton Tracking Irons." I have so many requests for them . . .*

If after perusal of my scheme for Boy Scouts you can say a good word for it in your lectures, I shall be very grateful indeed. It teaches stalking, observation, and love of animals.

Typed note by Ernest Thompson Seton:

In reply to B. P.'s letter of 13 Feb. 1908: I wrote

"Yes my tracking irons are copyrighted, but I give you special permission to manufacture fifty pairs, without royalty or other payment to me.

"Subsequent lots to be the subject of a new arrangement."

E. T. S.

This he acknowledges in his of 24 Feb. 1908 (see enclosed), but has continued to make and sell them, doubtless at a profit, ever since, 25 years at least, and has never made any accounting or a new arrangement. I (incog.) called at his B. S. headquarters in London, 1935, and bought a pair. The were sold to me as B. P. tracking irons.

E. T. Seton 1940.

March 2nd, 1908

My dear Seton:

I send you a copy of the parts of "Scouting for Boys" as far as they have been published to date . . .

March 14th 1908

Dear Seton:

Thank you very much for your kind letter. I much regret that I should have omitted mentioning the source of several of the games, as being taken from your "Birch-Bark Roll," but the truth is, I had made a general statement to that effect in the Introduction of the book, which afterwards cut out from the beginning and have inserted it at the end, where you will see it in Part IV. But in doing this I had not reflected that the remarks, giving authorship of the games, would not be read by the people until after the games had appeared before them. I very much regret this oversight, and it is most kind of you to have taken it in the good natured way in which you have done.

I am very much obliged to you for consenting to write a message for the paper, when you are already so fully occupied with other things.

I am very sorry that I have to be away in the North on the 27th, but your tickets will be very welcomed in my family, who will be there to hear you.

Typed note by Ernest Thompson Seton, undated, but probably from 1940:

On August 9th 1909 my publisher (Doubleday) through his agent H. C. Roberts protesting against the wholesale piracy of my work. To this B. P. replied 3 Sep.

3rd September, 1909

Mr. H. C. Roberts

Dear Sir,

In reply to yours of August 9th, I regret exceedingly that I should have omitted to state in the introduction to the Second Edition of "Scouting for Boys" that I had quoted some of the games from Mr. Ernest

Thompson Seton's book. I beg to point out that, so far from giving no credit whatever to that gentleman, I have in the beginning of the book stated which games were taken from his book, and also have mentioned him on pages 9, 18, 38, 70, 76, 91, 117, 139, 140, and 171. I hope that it will be seen from this that there was no intention on my part to pirate any of his excellent work, but that, on the contrary, I was anxious to advertise it and to make it more widely known to those interested in boys; and I hope that in this I have been unsuccessful. I am about to publish a book of Scouting and other games for boys, and if Mr. Thompson Seton would like me to further bring to notice his games and to draw attention to his book, I will gladly do so . . .

P. S. I may add that I have had many offers from the United States to publish our movement over there, and to start Scout organizations there, but I have always declined in order to avoid clashing with Mr. Thompson Seton's organization and work.

December 10th, 1909

My dear General:

Two months ago I sent you a letter of which the enclosed (Sep. 30) is a copy. As I have had no reply, I fear the letter has gone astray. Kindly let me hear from you at your earliest convenience, and oblige . . .

P. S. A friend of mine, to whom I have shown my letter, says that I have not made it perfectly clear what I think you should do to straighten this matter out. I will do so now. I think that you should come out frankly in the "Scout" and say that for many years Seton had been establishing boy's camps in America, in which the boys were taught scouting and woodcraft with a view to the development of character and, although this was done under the name of "Woodcraft Indiana," [sic] they were essentially the same as the "Boy Scouts" in England. One or two camps had already been formed in England, one of those being at Eccles with William Y. Knight as its leader.

Second. In 1904 I made an effort to spread the idea in England by lecturing on the subject at several points, notably London and Newcastle as well as Public Schools, and distributing the Birch Bark Roll of Camp Law to a great many of the head masters in England. I also wrote to Lord Roberts and to yourself about the matter. I wrote to you because you were the advocate of scouting in the army. I asked you to join with me in the undertaking and made a beginning by printing your name as Reviser of the Scouting Department in the seventh edition of the Birch Bark Roll, which appeared in 1908.

Third. You should admit that the scouting for boys was founded on my Birch Bark Roll in all essential features and a great many of its details are taken direct. If desired, I will furnish you with copies of my letters to you and to Lord Roberts, letters which long ante-date any of your publications on Scouting for boys.

Seton wrote at the top of the first page [of the original letter] "This letter sent 22 Dec. 09.

17th January 1910

Dear Thompson Seton,

I am much obliged to you for your letter of 10th December, enclosing a copy of a previous one, which I am extremely sorry to have left unanswered. I thought it was merely a reply to mine, and so left it without acknowledgement. For this I sincerely apologize.

I am, of course, glad to publish a statement, since you desire it, of my indebtedness to you for several details in "Scouting for Boys." I enclose herewith some paragraphs which I am inserting with the intent in "The Scout," and I hope that they will be satisfactory to you.

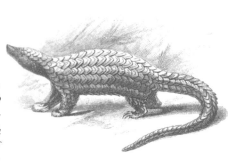

20th May, 1910

My dear Sir Robert:

I hear you are to be in Canada next August. I hope you will be able to visit us in camp in the Adirondacks (as per ancient promise), where we shall be during the month of August. We expect to have camps of both Scouts and Indians—several hundred, altogether—playing the game in the real wilderness. I am sure you will enjoy visiting us, and it will give us the greatest pleasure, so please promise you will come for at least one day. It is a short run from Montreal.

With congratulations on your success . . .

P. S. I am getting out a new edition of the Birch-Bark Roll in which I am incorporating Scouting for Boys as far as it serves this country, giving, of course, due credit. I hope this is agreeable to you.

[Ed. Note: Seton refers to the first publication of the new organization, Boy Scouts of America, Official Handbook, credited, "By Ernest Thompson Seton and Lieut.-Gen Sir S. S. Baden-Powell, K. C. B." Seton edited this book to combine part of the ninth Birch Bark Roll with part of Scouting for Boys. It seems to have been Seton's way of seeking reconciliation.]

May 31st, 1910

Dear Thompson Seton,

I am so very sorry to have left your note of 3rd March unanswered for such an unconscionable length of time, but I have been rather overdone with business and allowed it to get overlooked till a cable from Doubleday reminded me of it.

I have replied to his cable that - -

(1) I am sorry I cannot entirely confirm your entire statement:

(2) I have no knowledge of my book being produced in America by the International Press Service.

(3) but if it should be desirable and agreeable to you I would produce it in collaboration with you.

As regards (1) the statement you sent me, I cannot quite agree as to some of its deductions. For instance it never entered my head that I was going to assist your movement in England, because I never imagined that it would appeal to the English boy. (You say that you spoke on it at 15 centres in 1904 but only one took you it up.)

My scheme of Scouting was not based upon yours, but upon the system of training young soldiers by Scouting and badges which I employed in India in 1898–99. The book which I produced in 1900 for this was adopted by a number of schools and others for the instruction of boys. I then in 1908 rewrote it specially for the use of boys in the Boys Brigade etc., When I certainly took hints from you but also from Sir W. Smith and several other Authorities whom I consulted, and I included in it five of your games which I altered in some details and therefore in title, but giving the source from which I took them (mentioning you ten times in my book).

The final paragraph of your statement is so unfair to me that I had to qualify my approval of the statement as a whole; otherwise, without this, I should not much have objected to the rest, although somewhat misleading, as I don't care who has the credit so long as the boys get the training.

(2) I have consistently declined requests to start Boy Scouts in America, and have replied that your scheme already existed there. If my book has now been published there it is entirely without my knowledge or consent.

(3) At the same time it is evident to me that Boy Scouts will be started there—probably on a large scale—very shortly, because I am receiving letters from different parts of the United States asking how to start, etc. The Boy Scouts exist now in almost every country in the world except the U. S.

If therefore you think it would be desirable to meet what is evidently going to be a demand, I would gladly collaborate with you

in bringing out an American edition of my book through Messrs Doubleday or any other publisher you may select.

If you could rewrite such parts of it as requires it, to suit the American boy, I am sure the book would have a great success.

We can doubtless arrange terms that will be mutually satisfactory—as regards the profits.

I should be very glad indeed if we can arrange to work together.

June 7th, 1910

Dear Thompson Seton,

Thank you so much for your letter of the 20th May. I would like very much indeed to visit your Camp during August, as you suggest, if I can possibly get a day . . .

I had a talk with Roosevelt last night regarding the Boy Scouts and he is immensely keen on the subject and would, I no doubt [sic], take the Presidency [of the Boy Scouts] in the United States if desired.

12 Sept. 10. [letter sent by Baden-Powell to Doubleday Page and Co.]
Would you kindly let Mr. Thompson Ston [sic] know that I hope to be in New York on 23rd inst.—at the Waldorf—Astor [sic] sailing next day for England . . .
September 17, 1910

My dear Sir Robert:

I have just heard from Doubleday Page giving me your address. Doubtless you have heard from Robinson and Wakefield that we are giving you a private lunch and dinner . . . I am deputed to be the reception committee . . .

I ought to warn you there is some danger of a trap being laid for you in New York. You may have heard of Hearst, the socialist, anarchist, etc., who is largely responsible for the assassination of President McKinley. As soon as he found that the Boy Scouts was likely to take up, he started the American Boy Scouts as an advertising scheme for his American

Journal . . . It is quite likely he may have a deputation to meet you or call on you. If you do not know the man, ask anybody in Canada to tell you something about Hearst, who runs the New York Journal and The American. He had put the names of several of our executives in his paper in spite of their protests and threatened action and thus had collected quite a large sum that was meant for us.

24 Sept. 1910

My dear Thompson-Seton

I cannot leave without telling you how very sincerely gratified I have been by the exceedingly generous reception which has been accorded to me by yourself and those connected with the organization of the Boy Scout movement in the United States. I am, from the personal point of view, most deeply grateful—and from that movement I feel confident that in the hands of such capable workers and important backers as you have got together you are going to make a big success with the experiment.

Anything that I can do to help I will gladly do.

I had not, till I came here, exactly understood on what lines it was proposed that the scheme should be worked for the United States.

But since I have seen the excellent handbook which you have brought out and have realized that the movement is to be practically on the same lines as elsewhere I am only too glad to cooperate in any way that I can.

21st December, 1915

Dear Thompson Seton:

In reply to your letter, I should probably have no objection to your publishing, if you wish to do so, private letters which I wrote to you some eight or ten years ago; but it is a bit difficult to remember what I may have said

in them after such a lapse of time, and therefore must ask you kindly to let me see copies of them before I can acquiesce in their being made public.

As regards the assertion made by some of your papers that I considered the Board of the Boy Scouts justified in attacking you, I have certainly never authorized such a statement.

23rd October 1927

Dear Thompson Seton,

I do not remember having seen or written the History of Scouting to which you refer. You are correct in saying that I was glad to get some ideas from the Birch Bark Roll which you were good enough to give me in 1906 and I made acknowledgement of these in my book.

I cannot agree, however, that I got the main idea of Scouting from it as you appear to imply in the sixth paragraph of your letter. I had already been carrying out the principles for many years in the training of young soldiers in the Army.

If, however, you are anxious to claim authorship of the Boy Scout movement by all means do so. I have no objection, though I don't understand why, if you invented it, you have not carried it on.

The great thing, after all, is that it has come into being for the good of the boys.

August 8th 1939

Kenya Colony

Dear Thompson Seton

I have just received your letter of July the 17th, which was addressed to the Cavalry Club, London, and forwarded on to me by my secretary

Being away from home and from such letters as passed between us so many years ago, it is difficult for me to say whether I would approve, or not, their publication.

If you could kindly send me a copy of the extracts which you would propose to use, I could then definitely say yes or no. I hope that you will excuse the delay necessitated by me being here in East Africa.

How you would enjoy this country with its big game and beautiful scenery.

Appendix 4
The Seton Legacy

In her introduction to Robert Baden-Powell's Scouting for Boys, Elleke Boehmer included a couple of remarkable statistics—hidden in a footnote. Over the past century, Scouting has spread to nearly every country in the world, and during that time, the number of persons estimated to have participated in its programs has exceeded 350 million. The Boy Scouts of America has been the leading contributor to that number. The organization has counted over 111 million members between 1910 and 2006. Perhaps no other social movement outside of religious organizations can claim such a record. ETS, B-P, and Uncle Dan, for all their squabbling over who deserved credit for what, would have been amazed. Their work in service to youth was extraordinary. If there were a posthumous Nobel Prize for service to humankind, surely they would warrant the honor. Seton recognized children's inherent sense of curiosity—they want to learn and they want to connect with nature. Learning and connection are antidotes to a sense of separation and alienation. Woodcraft, and soon thereafter, Scouting, provided adults with the necessary means and methods to make kids feel connected to the world in a positive way.

Philmont Museum and Seton Memorial Library

There was almost nothing positive about the relationship between Seton and James West: the two never reconciled. But later, in 1965, Julia Seton and officials of the Boy Scouts of America resumed a dialogue after decades of silence. Julia, concerned about the continuance

of the Seton Legacy, wanted to find a way to keep "the Chief" from being forgotten. Correspondence included with the Seton Papers at Library and Archives Canada show that the initial discussion centered on a possible donation of Seton Castle and its collections to the National Council of the Boy Scouts of America. When that did not work, they came up with a second plan. In December 1965, Julia gifted most of Seton's personal library and artwork, plus natural history and Native American collections, for a museum built at Philmont Ranch, the great national camp of the Scouts in northern New Mexico. Located about halfway between Taos and the Currumpaw grasslands, the outstanding beauty of Philmont comes from its position astride the Cimarron Range of the Sangre de Cristo Mountains, where the Rockies meet the plains. Just as Philmont Ranch itself is at the meeting of two very different geographic worlds, the return of a connection between the Seton Legacy and the Boy Scouts was similarly dramatic. Whether or not Julia intended her gift as a gesture of reconciliation, it had that effect, for now the Scouts gave Seton a high degree of recognition at their flagship operation. L. O. Crosby Jr., of Picayune, Mississippi, a volunteer Scout, generously donated the funds needed to construct the Seton Memorial Library and Museum; it was dedicated at Philmont in ceremonies attended by Julia and top Scout officials on June 25, 1967. Built in a southwestern adobe style, the structure included two galleries, a library, two offices, a laboratory, and an underground storage facility. Initially, it served as the repository and exhibit area solely for the Seton collections.

By 1982, the museum's collections (and exhibitions) had expanded to include artifacts, memorabilia, books, and art related to the history, natural history, and native peoples of the Southwest, as well as that of Philmont and the Boy Scouts. To reflect the change in mission, its name was changed to the Philmont Museum and Seton Memorial Library. Today, the purpose of the Seton Memorial Library is to collect, preserve, and interpret the artifacts, memorabilia, and art of the co-founder of the Boy Scouts of America. Every year the Philmont Scout Ranch has over 22,000 Scouts participating in camping programs along with another 5,000 adult participants at the Philmont Training Center. Most of them visit the museum and library, where they see Seton's drawings and paintings.

The Academy for the Love of Learning

When, through Woodcraft and Scouting, Seton became the inspired creator of ground-breaking programs for, and in service to, young people, he helped lead the way into a century of deep thinking about how we approach the acquisition of knowledge. For Seton, the educational model of narrowly focusing a child's concentration on memorizing facts made no sense. (He would have been truly horrified at test-based learning such as the "No Child Left Behind" approach of the early twenty-first century.) Instead, he felt that education should encompass our whole being, beginning with establishing a healthy relationship to nature. The openness this engendered in the mind of a young person would lead him or her into a lifetime of learning. The purpose of education for Seton was not the production of cogs for the societal machine, but the nurturing of an inquiring and thoughtful mind. He wrote in the one-sentence Preface in *Two Little Savages* about the pursuit of knowledge: "Because I have known the torment of thirst, I would dig a well where others may drink." This was not a metaphoric quip; it was instead the very serious statement of a life's mission that he followed in teaching natural history and conservation, in promoting outdoor recreation and skills, and in fostering an appreciation for the values of Native America. In a career (and a personal life) filled with ups and downs, he never wavered from this calling as an educator.

The Academy for the Love of Learning began as an interconnected set of ideas coalescing at the end of the 1970s when its founder, Aaron Stern, recognized a growing crisis in education (the production of workers rather than the nurturing of learners). He had not heard of Seton or Woodcraft, but Seton's belief that the purpose of education was not scholarship but the development of character (out of which the greatest scholarship and the deepest values arise) was not too far off from the philosophy Stern was exploring. There are distinct differences between Seton's Woodcraft and Stern's approach; child development theory and educational models have changed a great deal in a hundred years. Yet, there is, as well, important common ground. The "Four-Fold Way" of Woodcraft calls for an integration of body, mind, spirit, and service; that is, a fully lived life is essentially holistic and ecological, in connection with nature, society, and other individuals. Woodcraft considered the individual (child or adult) not as a separate unit but as part of a larger system of male and female, of family, of community (to which service is owed), of spirituality, and of the natural world. Woodcraft stood against rigid standardization and instead believed that for each of us, a choice of our way in life should exist. Woodcraft felt that the competition that pits us against each other is morally wrong and that the beauty we find together in nature, or in our own creations (artistic or hand-crafted of whatever kind) is the highest good. Seton felt that the values he espoused were essential to the survival of our country and our civilization. Similarly, Stern has written:

> At the Academy's core has been a desire to bring to bear all of our capacities as human beings in an effort to revivify our natural impulse for learning and, thereby, over time, the way we go about educating. At stake, we feel, are the underpinnings of democracy itself, the very essence of which is an educated, awake, informed and engaged culture and citizenry.
>
> Even deeper are our simple longings to engage the fullness of our expressions as human beings on this planet—integrating our bodies, minds, emotions, and spirits with our personal destinies. We are, our selves, at risk, as is our planetary home.

Independently, Stern had come up with a concept almost identical to Seton's "Four-Fold Way." Seton wrote in *Blazes on the Trail* that "all boys [and girls!] are born good, are the children of God, and need only to be developed under sound leadership." Stern wrote, "In our work we open to the heart of learning itself and rest upon a deep trust that the seeds of basic goodness, love and learning live within all of us." Clearly, these two men should have known each other; they would have had a lot to talk about.

In a sense, that is what happened. The Academy for the Love of Learning was created from a ten-year collaboration between Stern and his mentor, Leonard Bernstein. Stern, then dean of the American Conservatory of Music in Chicago, explored aesthetic experience as a pathway into the kind of self-knowing and discovery that motivates and guides the natural human desire to learn. Before his death, Bernstein had posed a question for himself and Stern: Can we transform ourselves? Stern's continuing explorations and teaching (in New York and Nashville, among other places) led to the creation of the Academy. In the meantime, far away in New Mexico, Ernest and Julia's daughter, Dee Seton Barber, was thinking about another kind of transformation. Feeling deep responsibility for carrying on the Seton Legacy, Dee, with help from some like-minded

people, started a second Seton Institute. Her health problems, and the deteriorating condition of Seton Castle, led Dee to consider finding an organization that might take over the responsibility of continuing the Seton Legacy. She and Stern met through mutual acquaintances—she looking for help with the Castle and he looking for a base of operations for the Academy. A couple of conversations over a period of three years resulted in Stern traveling to Santa Fe, where the two of them discovered a deep connection between the philosophy of Seton and that of the Academy. For Stern, the key thought behind his work is "an absolute belief in the ability of the individual to transform," with learning as the means of transformation with a personal goal of "moving toward greater levels of contact with truth." Seton, like Stern, believed in working for personal and cultural transformation. In 2003, Seton Castle, along with its contents of Seton's remaining book and art collection (of his own artwork), came under the auspices of the Academy. Dee asked that the Academy include taking responsibility for continuing the Seton Legacy as part of its mission, a challenge that was accepted. (The 2010 Seton exhibition at the New Mexico History Museum in Santa Fe was an outcome of that process.)

The Academy soon began, and nearly completed, an extensive renovation of Seton Castle back to its appearance of the late 1930s. On November 15, 2005, a fire broke out during construction, utterly destroying the structure. A new, environmentally friendly building has been built adjacent to the Castle to house the programs of the Academy, including a gallery for display of Seton's artwork and a center for research on his life and work. The original outlines of the foundation and remaining walls of the Castle are being transformed to define a meditation garden. You can stand on the site where Ernest Thompson Seton, Julia Seton, and so many others once stood. Looking out across New Mexico from the last rampart of the Rockies, you can see just about forever.

Bibliography

Most of the primary source material for this book came from the Seton Papers, Library and Archives Canada, the national archives of Canada, located in Ottawa, National Capitol Region. Seton's extensive papers and records were maintained first by Julia Seton and later by Dee Barber Seton before Dee gave them to the archives in Ottawa. The author consulted the Seton Papers in October 2007. Quotes from the papers are used by kind permission of Library and Archives Canada.

Books and catalogs

Anderson, H. Allen. *The Chief: Ernest Thompson Seton and the Changing West.* College Station: Texas A&M Press, 1986.

Baden-Powell, Robert. *Scouting for Boys: A Handbook for Instruction in Good Citizenship.* Edited with an introduction and notes by Elleke Boehmer. Oxford: Oxford University Press, 2004.

Blassingame, Wyatt. *Ernest Thompson Seton: Scout and Naturalist.* Champaign, Illinois: Garrard Publishing Company, 1971.

Burke, Sir Richard. *A Genealogical History of the Dormant, Abegant, Forfeited, and Extinct Peerages of the British Empire.* London: Harrison, 1883.

Chapman, Frank M. *Bird-Life: A Guide to the Study of Our Common Birds.* New York: D. Appleton and Company, 1897.

Churchill, Winston. *A History of the English Speaking Peoples.* Vol. 1, *The Birth of Britain.* New York: Bantam, 1956.

Garland, Hamlin. *Companions on the Trail: A Literary Chronicle.* New York: Macmillan, 1931.

———. *My Friendly Contemporaries: A Literary Log.* New York: Macmillan, 1932.

Garst, Shannon, and Warren Garst. *Ernest Thompson Seton: Naturalist.* New York: Julian Messner, 1959.

Gray, Charlotte. *Flint & Feather: The Life and Times of E. Pauline Johnson, Tekahionwake.* Toronto: Harper Flamingo Canada, 2002.

Gray, D. J. *William Wallace: The King's Enemy.* New York: Barnes & Noble Books, 1991.

James, William. *The Varieties of Religious Experience.* New York: Penguin, 1982.

Keller, Betty. *Black Wolf: The Life of Ernest Thompson Seton.* Toronto: Douglas & McIntyre, 1984.

Kuhn, Thomas. *The Structure of Scientific Revolutions.* Chicago: The University of Chicago Press, 1962.

Leopold, Aldo. *A Sand County Almanac.* London: Oxford University Press, 1949.

Lutts, Ralph H. *The Nature Fakers: Wildlife, Science and Sentiment.* Golden, CO: Fulcrum, 1990.

Mason, Bernard S. *Dances and Stories of the American Indian.* New York: A. S. Barnes, 1944.

McNamee, Colm. *The Wars of the Bruces: Scotland, England, and Ireland, 1306–1328.* East Lothian, Scotland: Tuckwell, 1997.

Morris, Brian. *Ernest Thompson Seton, Founder of the Woodcraft Movement, 1860–1946: Apostle of Indian Wisdom and Pioneer Ecologist.* New York: Edwin Mellen, 2007.

Muir, John. *My First Summer in the Sierra*, in *Nature Writings.* New York: Library of America, 1997.

Murray, William D. *The History of the Boy Scouts of America.* New York: Boy Scouts of America, 1937.

Pakenham, Thomas. *The Boer War.* London: Abacus, 1992.

Pond, J. B. *Eccentricities of Genius: Memories of Famous Men and Women of the Platform and Stage.* New York: G. W. Dillingham, 1900.

Redekop, Magdalene. "Ernest Thompson Seton." In *The Canadians.* Don Mills, Ontario: Fitzhenry & Whiteside, 1979.

Robertson, Edna, and Sarah Nestor. *Artists of the Canyons and Caminos: Santa Fe, the Early Years*. Salt Lake City: Gibbs Smith, 1982.

Samson, John G., ed. *The Worlds of Ernest Thompson Seton*. New York: Knopf, 1976.

Schmitt, Peter J. *Back to Nature: The Arcadian Myth in Urban America*. New York: Oxford University Press, 1969.

Seton, Grace Gallatin. *A Woman Tenderfoot*. New York: Doubleday, 1900.

———. *Nimrod's Wife*. London: Constable, 1907.

Seton, Julia M. *By a Thousand Fires: Nature Notes and Extracts from the Life and Unpublished Journals of Ernest Thompson Seton*. New York: Doubleday, 1967.

———. *Trail and Camp-Fire Stories*. New York: D. Appleton-Century, 1940.

Seton, Robert. *An Old Family, Or, The Setons of Scotland and America*. New York: Bretano's, 1899.

Smith, Pamela S. *Passions in Print: Private Press Artistry in New Mexico, 1834–Present*. With Richard Polese. Santa Fe: Museum of New Mexico Press, 2006.

Steffens, Lincoln. *The Autobiography of Lincoln Steffens*. New York: Harcourt, Brace and Company, 1931.

Stickney, J. H. *Bird World: A Bird Book for Children*. Assisted by Ralph Hoffman. Boston: Ginn, 1902.

Taylor, Maurice. *Bulletin in Bold Characters: A Bibliography of Seton Village Press*. Santa Fe: Press of the Palace of the Governors, Museum of New Mexico, 1990.

Thompson, Austin Seton. *Spadina: A Story of Old Toronto*. Toronto: Pagurian, 1975.

Thoreau, Henry David. *Collected Essays And Poems*. New York: Library of America, 2001.

Van Slyck, Abigail A. *A Manufactured Wilderness: Summer Camps and the Shaping of American Youth, 1890–1960*. Minneapolis: University of Minnesota Press, 2006.

Wadland, John. *Ernest Thompson Seton: Man in Nature and the Progressive Era, 1880–1915*. New York: Arno, 1978.

Wiley, Farida, ed. *Ernest Thompson Seton's America: Selections from the Writings of the Artist-Naturalist*. New York: Devin-Adair, 1954.

Journals, periodicals, newspaper articles, and miscellaneous publications and sources

Arnold, John. "House of Knowledge." *Albuquerque Journal North*, November 11, 2003.

Avellar, Raphael. "It Isn't at All Remarkable That He's a Father at 78, Says Ernest Seton, Planning Another Child Soon." *New York World-Telegram*, November 19, 1938.

Bacon, Lucy. "Seton Village." *New Mexico*, July 1933.

Bolt, Penny. "Seton's Indians." Oral history interview with Leonard S. Clark. Greenwich: Greenwich Library, 1976.

"Boy Scouts Honor Founders." *Kansas City Times*, February 10, 1941.

"Boys Play on Seton Estate." *New York Herald*, October 18, 1903.

Conservation Hall of Fame. See National Wildlife Federation: www.nfw.org.

Emlen, George. "Seton, the man and the village." *New Mexican*, July 2, 1977.

"E. Thompson Seton, Noted Author, Dies." *New York Times*, October 24, 1946.

"Ernest Thompson Seton." *Evening Star*, October 25, 1946.

"Ernest Thompson Seton." *The Museum Review*, published by the State Historical Society of North Dakota, January 1947, Vol. 2, No. 1.

"Famed Naturalist Awaits Birth of Child." *New Mexican*, June 11, 1938.

Forcey, Pamela. "Grace Gallatin Seton." Newsletter, Historical Society of the Town of Greenwich, Winter 1994.

Fowler, Glenn. "Anya Seton, Author of 'Foxfire' and Other Novels, Is Dead at 86." *New York Times*, November 10, 1990.

Griffith, Dorsey. "Property owners jumpy over assessments." *New Mexican*, June 4, 1988.

"Happy Hunting Ground." *Time*, November 4, 1946.

Macintyre, F. Beatrice. "The Paleface Chief." *New Mexico*, April 1948.

MacKethan, Lucinda H., John R. Van Atta, and Kirsten M. Jensen. *Greenwich History* 7 (2002).

"Mrs. Seton Denies Story of Child." *New Mexican*, June 13, 1938.

"Pasadenans Mourn Passing of Ernest Thompson Seton, Noted Nature-Author." *Star News*, October 23, 1946.

Patterson, Stuart. "My First Eighty Years" and other writings and letters regarding his knowledge of Seton in 1893, estate of Edgar L. Moss, courtesy of Patricia Loughridge Appraisal Services.

Randles, Slim. "Historical Treasures, Seton Castle Basement Yields Box of Writings." *Albuquerque Journal*, February 3, 1994.

Roybal, Chris. "Hoping to restore history." *New Mexican*, August 7, 1995.

"Seton Institute, Summer School and Camp." Promotional brochure, ca. 1936.

"Seton Still Insists on Quitting Scouts." *New York Times*, December 6, 1915.

"Seton Village: a man's memorial." *New Mexican*, July 3, 1966.

"Seton's Ashes Strewn in N. M." *Chicago Daily Tribune*, August 15, 1960.

Sharpe, Tom. "California-based nonprofit to buy Seton Castle." *New Mexican*, March 31, 2002.

"United States Statutes at Large." Vol. 38, Part 2, pp. 1960–1964. Protection of migratory birds, an act making appropriations for the Department of Agriculture (the Weeks-McLean law).

"Visit Historic Seton Castle." Promotional brochure, 1950s.

Wallace, Ralph. "Wild Animals He Has Known." *Readers' Digest* 49 (September 1946): 59–63.

"West Says Seton Is Not a Patriot." *New York Times*, December 7, 1915.

"World Lectures, Ernest Thompson Seton, Julia M. Seton & Beulah Seton." Promotional brochure, ca. 1941.

Zollars, Jerry. "Ernest Thompson Seton's Life in New Mexico." Unpublished manuscript, June 11, 2005, provided to David L. Witt and the Academy for the Love of Learning by Jerry Zollars.

Publications by Ernest Thompson Seton

Sources consulted for this study by Ernest Thompson Seton (aka Ernest Seton-Thompson), showing the edition used, are listed below. Seton's work has been issued in multiple editions, leading to a variety of guesses as to the number of original books he actually published. This list does not show all of the various editions.

Animal Heroes: Every Boy's Library—Boy Scout Edition. New York: Charles Scribner's Sons, 1905.

The Arctic Prairies. New York: Charles Scribner's Sons, 1911.

Bannertail: The Story of a Gray Squirrel. New York: Charles Scribner's Sons, 1922.

The Biography of an Arctic Fox. New York: Applegate-Century, 1937.

The Biography of a Grizzly. New York: Grosset & Dunlap, 1927. First published as a series in *Century* magazine in 1899.

The Biography of a Silver Fox. New York: Century, 1909.

Blazes on the Trail, No. 1: Lifecraft or Woodcraft. Greenwich, CT: Woodcraft League, 1928.

Blazes on the Trail, No. 2: Rise of the Woodcraft Indians. Greenwich, CT: Woodcraft League, 1928.

Blazes on the Trail, No. 3: Spartans of the West. Santa Fe: Woodcraft League, 1930.

The Book of Woodcraft and Indian Lore. New York: Doubleday, 1913. Reprinted in similar form in 1923 and other editions. Republished as *Ernest Thompson Seton's Big Book of Country Living*. New York: Lyons Press, 2000.

Boy Scouts of America Handbook. Proof copy of the 1st edition. New York: Doubleday, 1911.

The Buffalo Wind. Santa Fe: Seton Village Press, 1938.

The Foresters Manual, Or, The Forest Trees of Eastern North America. No. 2 of the Scout Manual Series. New York: Doubleday, 1912. Also published in *The Book of Woodcraft* (1923) as the chapter "Forestry."

The Gospel of the Redman. Santa Fe: Seton Village, 1937.

Great Historic Animals, Mainly About Wolves. New York: Charles Scribner's Sons, 1937.

"How to Catch Wolves with the Newhouse Wolf Trap." *Oneida Community* (New York), *Limited,* with an essay, "Wolf Trapping," by Seton, undated, but from 1890s.

How to Play Indian. Philadelphia: Curtis, 1903.

Journal V. Original manuscript owned by the American Museum of Natural History in New York.

"The King of Currumpaw, A Wolf Story." *Scribner's Magazine* 16, No. 5, 618–628.

Life Histories of Northern Animals. 2 vols. New York: Charles Scribner's Sons, 1909.

Lives of Game Animals. Vol. 1, *Cats, Wolves, and Foxes.* New York: Doubleday, 1925.

Lives of Game Animals. Vol. 2, *Bears, Coons, Badgers, Skunks, and Weasels.* New York: Doubleday, 1926.

Lives of Game Animals. Vol. 3, *Hoofed Animals.* New York: Doubleday, 1927.

Lives of Game Animals. Vol. 4, *Rodents, etc.* New York: Doubleday, 1928.

Lives of the Hunted. New York: Charles Scribner's Sons, 1901.

Lobo, Rag, and Vixen. New York: Charles Scribner's Sons. Another edition, not from the Scribner Series of School Reading, was printed without a date. The book was a reprinting of four earlier published stories.

Manual of the Woodcraft Indians. New York: Doubleday, 1915.

Monarch: The Big Bear of Tallac. New York: Charles Scribner's Sons, 1904.

The Nature Library: Animals. New York: Doubleday, 1926. This work consists of selections from *Life Histories of Northern Animals.*

The Preacher of Cedar Mountain: A Tale of the Open Country. New York: Doubleday, 1917.

Rolf in the Woods. New York: Grosset & Dunlap, 1911. Reprinted as part of *The Library of Pioneering and Woodcraft.* New York: Doubleday, 1926.

The Red Lodge. Undated Woodcraft League pamphlet, ca. 1915.

Santana, the Hero Dog of France. Los Angeles: Phoenix Press, 1945.

Studies in the Art Anatomy of Animals. London: Macmillan, 1896.

The Ten Commandments in the Animal World. New York: Doubleday, 1923. First published as *The Natural History of the Ten Commandments.* New York: Charles Scribner's Sons, 1907.

Trail of an Artist-Naturalist: The Autobiography of Ernest Thompson Seton. New York: Charles Scribner's Sons, 1940.

The Trail of the Sandhill Stag. New York: Charles Scribner's Sons, 1901.

The Trail of the Sandhill Stag and Other Lives of the Hunted. New York: Dutton, 1966. Stories compiled from several earlier books by Seton.

Two Little Savages. New York: Doubleday, 1903. Reprinted in several later editions.

Wild Animals at Home. New York: Doubleday, 1913. Reprinted in 1913, 1917, and 1923.

Wild Animals I Have Known. New York: Charles Scribner's Sons, 1898.

Wild Animal Ways. New York: Doubleday, 1916.

Woodland Tales. New York: Doubleday, 1921.

Woodmyth & Fable. New York: Century, 1905.

Notes

Chapter 1

5   *"The King of Currumpaw, A Wolf Story"* Seton began working on "Lobo" in February 1894, shortly after his return from New Mexico. He sold the story to the magazine in May. It was the lead in the short-story collection *Wild Animals I Have Known.*

13   *"How to Catch Wolves"* Undated wolf-trap sales brochure. Seton is listed as "Government Naturalist of Manitoba," a position he officially obtained in November 1892. Philmont Museum and Seton Memorial Library archive.

14   *Stuart Hayt Patterson* These accounts are from Patterson's personal archives. His autobiography, along with letters to, from, or about Seton were preserved by one of his relatives, Edgar L. Moss of Richmond, Virginia, who died in 2007. The papers were found by Ellen Firsching Brown (Liberty Hall Books) and Patricia Loughridge, ISI (Patricia Loughridge Appraisal Services), also both of Richmond. They very kindly provided the author with the documents, including "My First Eighty Years," by Stuart Hayt Patterson, Retired Vice President and Comptroller of the Guaranty Trust Company of New York—and former Texas and New Mexico cowboy. Patterson's accounts of his times in New York, California, and Texas are taken from that manuscript.

15   *Lewis V. Fitz Randolph* His name has been shown by other scholars as "Fitz-Randolph." In his letters to Patterson, the ranch owner signed himself as "L.V. Fitz Randolph"—no hyphen.

16   *I have decided* Letter from Seton to Fitz Randolph, October 6, 1893, from Journal V, ETS.

17   *"I have just received"* Letter from Fitz Randolph to Patterson, October 10, 1863, Patterson archive.

18   *A couple of weeks later* "My First Eighty Years," Patterson archive.

18   *Seton had a great mass of hair* Ibid.

20   *"Hubert, unless thou turnest"* C. F. Wemyss Brown, trans. H. Jon Thomas, *The Catholic Encyclopedia,* Vol. VII. New York: Robert Applegate Company, 1910. Online at www.newadvent.org

21   *The Revival* This is part of a larger manuscript, "History of the Woodcraft Movement." There are various versions; the one used here was probably typed in the 1930s. Seton Papers, Library and Archives Canada.

23   *it became my habit* Seton titled this account of his trip to the Southwest "Four Months in New Mexico." Undated document, Seton Papers, Library and Archives Canada.

25   *a check for $80* A calculation made by Pamela Forcey on the Web site www.measuringworth.com showed that $80 in late 1893 would be the approximate equivalent of $2000 in early 2008.

25   *You will recall* Letter from A. W. Thompson to Seton, December 21, 1943. Seton Papers, Library and Archives Canada.

30   *He gave it the number 653* This number refers to the number of mammal specimens included in Seton's catalog; that is, he had killed or received into his collection a total of 653 mammals. Bird specimens were numbered separately.

36   *We have a thought* James, *The Varieties of Religious Experience,* 193–97.

37   *At least some part* The author joined Big Tree researcher and photographer Robert Hare for a two-week intensive exploration of the California redwood and sequoia forests in 2005. He brought

JACK
IN
A
PULPIT

to the author's attention the importance of naming wild creatures.

38 *Reviewing his New Mexico journal* Copies of Journal V and the rest of Seton's journals are at the Philmont Museum and Seton Memorial Library. All the original journals are at the American Museum of Natural History in New York City.

Chapter 2

42 *"clad in the preposterous"* Seton, *Trail of an Artist-Naturalist*, 7. All the quotations in the text noted as from his autobiography are from this book.

43 *"I see yet"* Ibid., 11.

43 *Father came prepared* Ibid., 12.

44 *"the sweet and holy"* Ibid., 12.

44 *"taught me to read"* Kate Stevenson, great-great-granddaughter of Agnes O'Brien (née O'Leary), e-mail of October 31, 2005, to Ronald L. Edmonds, Seton researcher, who shared it with the author.

45 *"the joy Balboa had"* Seton, *Trail of an Artist-Naturalist*, 102.

46 *His heart was more* Seton, *Two Little Savages*, 56. This is one of many editions of the book, which was first published in 1903.

47 *The result* The painting barely survived the decades, but, cleared of layers of grime, came to life again after restoration by the Academy for the Love of Learning.

48 *Anne Arthurs* Thompson, *Spadina*, 202–3. The house, now known as the Spadina Museum, was one of the greatest mansions built in nineteenth-century Toronto.

50 *"The Plan of My Life"* Dated "March 7th, 1881." Seton Papers, Library and Archives Canada.

55 *"The Winnipeg Wolf"* Seton, *Animal Heroes*.

56 *"personality, sex, condition"* Seton, *Trail of an Artist-Naturalist*, 210.

68 *Seton sold the painting* Seton, letter to W. W. Stewart, November 20, 1895. The letter, showing Seton's address of the time as 9 rue Campagne Première, discusses the possible sale of a "wolf picture." He asked Stewart (who is unidentified and

could have been either the buyer or a dealer) if he could keep a photographic negative of the image. He did publish a photograph of this painting in his autobiography, opposite p. 286. Also, there is no indication that he returned to Canada with the painting. This letter, then, may represent sales documentation of *Sleeping Wolf.*

69 *Naturalist for the Province* David Philip, Chief Clerk, letter to Seton, November 16, 1892. Library and Archives Canada.

Chapter 3

72 *Seton nearly missed the boat* Seton, *Trail of an Artist-Naturalist*, 343. Seton also noted in his Journal 2 his near miss getting onboard, adding, "on boat met Miss G Gallatin."

72 *When the ship set out* In a letter from Caroline Fitz Randolph to Seton, March 13, 1895, she wrote, "At last the head of your victim has come, am very proud of it and delighted I am. It is the very best thing of its kind that I have ever seen, and I am already attached to it as the glory of my modest possessions." He also noted in his Journal 2 that he had sent two wolf skins to Fitz Randolph in April and May.

73 *I have spent* Pine statement, transcribed from original dated December 22, 1894. Seton Papers, Library and Archives Canada. The first reader of this catalog, artist-naturalist Robert G. Hare, commented on the pine statement: "Seton was fortunate to discover this wisdom at his young age. I don't think his pine stands for a particular endeavor but rather that whatever he does and how he does it comes from WHO HE IS (his innate pine soul) rather than what he thinks others would like (the palm). Thus "the man who does immortal work develops himself." It is what will grow in HIS soil—the soil of his soul or inner nature. At an important level he gave up immature approval-seeking and found

himself." Robert G. Hare to author, e-mail, January 16, 2008.

75 *So when, the year after* Grace Gallatin Seton, *A Woman Tenderfoot*, 1.

76 *"As soon as I saw"* Seton, *Trail of an Artist-Naturalist*, 329. The Seton papers at Library and Archives Canada include a curious unpublished manuscript, "The Visit of Satan," a quasi-fictional account of Seton's life in Manitoba during the 1880s, in which Seton defended himself with a knife against a railroad worker. The incident could have turned deadly; Seton at least presents himself as willing to kill during that fight. Had he attended, the party in Clayton could once more have forced him into violence. Although he was like most North Americans of his time—anti-war in his beliefs—Seton was not a pacifist, but avoiding a fight he knew was coming was sensible. His cowboy-killer friend saw things differently.

77 *"no glory in the achievement"* Grace Gallatin Seton, *A Woman Tenderfoot*, 85, 95. After her separation from Seton, Grace continued big-game hunting from time to time.

77 *"The heat and glare"* Ibid., 255, 262–63.

77 *"Badlands Billy, The Wolf That Won"* This story was originally published in two parts as "Billy, the Big Wolf," in the August and September 1905 issues of *Ladies' Home Journal*. It was republished under the new title in *Animal Heroes*.

82 *"Are we to believe"* A comprehensive account is found in Lutts, *The Nature Fakers*.

83 *An opportunity* Seton gives his account in *Trail of an Artist-Naturalist*, 367–71.

84 *While Roosevelt did not* Roosevelt's article was published in *Everybody's Magazine* 17, September 1907, 427–30. Citation of this article appears in Lutts, *The Nature Fakers*.

85 *As stories based* Garland, *Companions on the Trail*, 205.

86 *Seton described it* Seton, *Wild Animals At Home*. A somewhat longer version of the account is found in the section "The Moose I Called," in *Lives of Game Animals*, Vol. 3, 225–27.

87 *"a colorless record"* Seton quoted his original writing from *The Arctic Prairies* and the new account of his feelings in *Lives of Game Animals*, Vol. I, 198.

88 *a similar experience* Leopold, *A Sand County Almanac*, 176.

88 *"Truly, it is a grand Work"* Hornaday to Seton, November 26, 1909. Seton Papers, Library and Archives Canada.

88 *Seton had to turn it down* Seton to Hornaday, December 9, 1909. Seton Papers, Library and Archives Canada.

88 *I have read* Theodore Roosevelt to Seton, January 6, 1911. Seton Papers, Library and Archives Canada.

89 *Mr. Henry Ford* Glen Buck to Seton, December 18, 1912. Seton Papers, Library and Archives Canada.

89 *Seton considered the legislation* Seton, *Trail of an Artist-Naturalist*, 371. The Weeks-McLean Act, 37 Stat. 847, is found in *Statutes at Large*, Vol. 38, Part 2, 1913–1915, 1960–64, United States Code. Its first paragraph is important enough to include here: "All wild geese, wild swans, brant, wild ducks, snipe, plover, woodcock, rail, wild pigeons, and all other migratory game and insectivorous birds which in their northern and southern migrations pass through or do not remain permanently the entire year within the borders of any State or Territory, shall hereafter be deemed to be within the custody and protection of the Government of the United States, and shall not be destroyed or taken contrary to regulations hereinafter provided therefor."

89 *"An Account of"* Seton, *Lives of Game Animals*, title page.

90 *I had some sorrows* Seton to Frank M. Chapman, April 12, 1930. Seton Papers, Library and Archives Canada.

91 *"Did human hand"* Ibid., 66.

Chapter 4

98 *a hundred acres* Seton, *Trail of an Artist-Naturalist*, 376.

98 *"2 Little Savages"* Seton, Journal 8, 6. Philmont Museum.

98 *"wicked pictures"* Seton, *Blazes on the Trail, No. 2*, 3–13. Seton did not record the exact date of the first camp, but it may have occurred on Easter weekend. If so, the dates were March 28 and 29.

99 *His most daring move* Ethnic nomenclature, malleable over time, follows two tracks, one of words used by, in this case, white society, and another used by indigenous peoples. In this work, the author has tried to use terms in the appropriate context, such as First Nations for Indians in Canada; Indians, for the original inhabitants of the Western United States; and Native America, for American Indian peoples collectively. In Seton's book title *Two Little Savages*, the meaning is clear: two white boys play at being Indians (savages)—as inappropriate then as now, but still in common use in Seton's time. When Seton called himself a "Medicine Man" of the Woodcraft "Indians," he meant the term to be seen as honorific. The "tribes" of white boys sometimes took the names of displaced American Indian tribes—hardly an honor to those original inhabitants who had lost their homes. "Redman" and "Red Indians" were colloquialisms of the time also used by Seton. Does this show honoring of Indians on Seton's part or merely cultural appropriation? Opinions will vary on this point, but in our consideration of him, we should consider that he continually acknowledged that the Woodcraft movement was based on tribal ethics and standards (as he understood them). In *Gospel of the Redman*, Seton made clear that he had submitted the manuscript for critique by Indians, including his friend Dr. Charles A. Eastman. Correspondence in Seton's papers show his continuing commitment to Native rights; that is, for all his admiration of the historical Indian, he was concerned as well with the living peoples of his time. By the time Seton published *Gospel of the Redman*,

he no longer employed the word "savages"; the Indians he wrote about were "Prophets." Over time his attitudes seem to have evolved in a more sensitive way.

100 *By coincidence* The coincidence of the publication of the "Seton's Boys" articles was described by Seton in his unpublished history of the Woodcraft movement, 17. Seton Papers, Library and Archives Canada. *Ladies' Home Journal* was an influential publication giving Seton's ideas more exposure than he could have received anywhere else.

100 *"Went to Summit"* Seton Journal 11, 90. Philmont Museum. In the twenty-first edition of the *Birch Bark Roll of Woodcraft*, published in 1927, Seton wrote, "On the first of July, at Summit, N. J., I founded the first tribe that I personally led," but in *Blazes on the Trail* (1928) he emphasized that first camping weekend in Cos Cob three months earlier.

100 *"the study of Woodcraft"* "Seton Indians," publicity flyer from lecture promoter J. B. Pond, advertising a Seton lecture at the Carnegie Lyceum on February 21, 1903.

101 *An Indian uprising* "Are You A Seton Indian? Whoop!" *New York Herald*, October 11, 1903.

103 *"The best things"* Seton, *How to Play Indian*, 3. Impersonation of Indians lives on in a very limited way in a Boy Scout honorary society, the Order of the Arrow, a direct ancestor of the Seton Indians.

103 *Its wood* From the *New York Herald*, October 11, 1903. Additional detail from the *New York Herald*, October 18, 1903, "Boys Play on Seton Estate."

104 *Most boys* Seton, *How to Play Indian*, 3.

105 *Like other educators* Seton was familiar with the work of Russian philosopher Peter Kropotkin, who believed in a theory of "mutual aid" in the successful organization of society, an outgrowth of Charles Darwin's observations about nature. Kropotkin's ideas are discussed in Wadland, *Ernest Thompson Seton*, chapters 1 and 5.

106 *"the main point"* "Indians At Wyndygoul," *Greenwich News*, October 23, 1903. Philmont Archive. And in Morris, *Ernest Thompson Seton*, 193–96. Morris interviewed White on August 21, 1976. Leonard Clark recalled that the first camp occurred on Easter weekend, but with fewer boys than claimed by Seton. Also see Anderson, *The Chief*, 285.

107 *"Whether we owe allegiance"* Seton's typescript of Beard's announcement, May 1905. Seton Papers, Library and Archives Canada.

108 *The war against the Boers* See Pakenham, *The Boer War*.

109 *Revisionist historians* Robert Baden-Powell and Elleke Boehmer, *Scouting for Boys: The Original 1908 Edition* (New York: Oxford University Press, 2004). This reissued edition includes annotations by Elleke Boehmer mentioning Seton's contributions to Baden-Powell's book, plus new scholarship on B-P. See also Morris, *Ernest Thompson Seton*, chapter 5.

111 *"It is exactly the sort of thing"* Seton to Baden-Powell, November 3, 1906. Seton Papers, Library and Archives Canada.

111 *Instead of addressing the issue* Baden-Powell to Seton, March 14, 1908. Seton Papers, Library and Archives Canada.

112 *Boyce incorporated* There are several accounts covering the first months of the Boy Scouts. One of the most detailed is in Anderson, *The Chief*, chapter 15.

114 *There is serious work* Hornaday to Seton, June 28, 1910. Seton Papers, Library and Archives Canada.

115 *I wish it were possible* Roosevelt to Seton, September 13, 1910. Seton Papers, Library and Archives Canada.

115 *The general was magnanimous* "Boy Scouts Honor Founders," *Kansas City Times*, February 10, 1941. This story was repeated in print a number of times from when it was first printed in 1910. Thirty-one years later, reporters were still using it. Seton Papers, Library and Archives Canada.

117 *Seton wrote an introduction* Proof copy of the 1st Edition of the *Boy Scouts of America Handbook* (New York: Doubleday, 1911). From the collection of the Academy for the Love of Learning. Various authors are listed, including Seton, who is credited for "A Message from the Chief Scout" and for sections on Woodlore, Mushrooms, Trees, Wild Animals; Tracks, Trailing, and Signaling; and Indoor and Outdoor Games. Terminology such as "original edition" and "1st edition" may not be entirely familiar even to Scouters, let alone anyone else. The Boy Scout handbooks moved through many incarnations over the years. For a guide to the intricacies of the publication history and details about each of the editions, see *The Boy Scout Handbook, 1910–Today*, a monograph by Jeff Snowden, Scoutmaster, Troop 97 BSA, at www.troop97.net/bshb1.htm.

118 *The attitude* Wadland, *Ernest Thompson Seton*, 423–28. Wadland points out that control of the Boy Scouts of America devolved from its initial incorporator, W. D. Boyce, and his surrogate, Executive Board President Colin Livingstone, who was entrusted with putting the board under the control of Republican businessmen. Not surprisingly, they favored the Baden-Powell vision of Scouting over that of Seton, giving West free rein to run the Boy Scouts along the lines of the English model.

120 *His publisher* Ibid., 439.

121 *For Roosevelt* Keller, *Black Wolf.* Keller quotes from *The Letters of Theodore Roosevelt*, ed. Elting Morison (Cambridge: Harvard University Press, 1951).

121 *O come off* Beard to Seton, November 30, 1915. Seton Papers, Library and Archives Canada. This blow-up between Beard and Seton is also noted in Morris, *Ernest Thompson Seton*, 233.

123 *An unattributed article* The *Boys' Life* article is quoted in Wadland, *Ernest Thompson Seton*, 442.

124 *The eleventh edition* Seton, *The Book of Woodcraft and Indian Lore.* The Woodcraft League opened its first office in New York City in December 1915.

125 *As I sat* Garland, *My Friendly Contemporaries,* 104.

125 *Concerning the Woodcraft League* Seton to Frank M. Chapman, April 12, 1930. Seton Papers, Library and Archives Canada.

126 *"Compulsionists"* Seton, *Blazes on the Trail,* 4–5.

128 *"Our watchword"* Seton, *The Book of Woodcraft and Indian Lore,* 61.

Chapter 5

130 *This beneficial partnership* See *The Autobiography of Lincoln Steffens* (New York: Harcourt, 1931), 440. Steffens noted the essential importance of Grace on Seton's career.

132 *"You can't give"* "Seton's Indians," Leonard S. Clark, oral history interview conducted by Penny Bolt (Greenwich, CT: Greenwich Library, 1976).

134 *her first meeting with Seton* Julia Seton gave her version of their first encounter in Ernest Thompson Seton's *Trail and Camp-Fire Stories,* ix.

134 *they met after the lecture* Therese La Farge, "The Indefatigable, Indestructible Julia Seton," *Santa Fe News,* October 9, 1969. Quoted in Anderson, *The Chief,* 204.

135 *They traveled to Santa Fe* Julia Seton described the founding and early days of Seton Village in a 1955 interview, a transcript of which is in the Seton Papers, Library and Archives Canada. Apparently the interview was conducted with Julia at Seton Castle, but the transcript does not name the interviewer, nor does it give the intended use or publication of the interview.

136 *when we stood together* Julia Seton, *By a Thousand Fires,* 253.

136 *At the same time* I am indebted to Seton Village resident Jerry Zollars, who has put together a narrative chronology of the development from its beginning in 1930. He made available to me

his unpublished manuscript, "Ernest Thompson Seton's Life in New Mexico, Notes taken from his daily Journal and other sources," June 11, 2005.

137 *a habitable stage* Seton completed the main work on the Castle in 1939.

137 *For camp directors* From *The Totem Board,* May 1934. This newsletter was an occasional publication of the Woodcraft League. An undated brochure, "Seton Institute, Summer School and Camp," possibly from around 1936, gives additional details. Copies of this promotional material were given to the Academy for the Love of Learning by Dieter Rall, a Santa Fe resident who attended the summer camp when he was a boy. Julia Seton wrote about the summer program in *By a Thousand Fires,* 261–62. The College of Indian Wisdom began its first summer program in 1932. The name changed to "Seton Institute—A School for Indian Life" in October 1935 and continued as an annual event through the summer of 1940, after which it was discontinued.

139 *As with the original Seton Indians* Elizabeth Lane Coulter, personal correspondence to author, September 6, 2006. Mrs. Coulter provided some details about the camp. She and her husband Frank worked at the summer camp "to care for and entertain the children" during the 1930s.

139 *"tears would come to his eyes"* Dieter Rall, interview with author, June 13, 2006.

141 *They published* "World Lectures, Ernest Thompson Seton, Julia M. Seton and Beulah Seton," self-published promotional brochure, c. 1941.

141 *Maurice had come* Taylor, *Bulletin in Bold Characters,* 7–9.

143 *In regard* Beard to Seton, April 13, 1935. Seton Papers, Library and Archives Canada. Also: Beard to Seton, March 27, 1935.

143 *Well, well* Seton to Beard, June 3, 1935. Seton Papers, Library and Archives Canada.

144 *the Setons refused a condition* Zollars, "Ernest

Thompson Seton's Life in New Mexico." Zollars pieced together the Setons' adoption plans from a careful reading of Seton's final journals.

144 *On their way back* Hot Springs was renamed Truth or Consequences in 1950 after the popular Ralph Edwards radio show (later, also a hit television series). Edwards offered to broadcast his show from any town that would rename itself after his show. Today, New Mexicans often refer to the small town as "T or C." The Carrie Tingley Hospital was named after the wife of a New Mexico governor who was instrumental in establishing a facility in New Mexico specializing in the treatment of polio in children. Hot Springs, as its name suggests, was, like Warm Springs, Georgia (made famous by Franklin D. Roosevelt), a place where naturally heated thermal waters were thought to contain special healing properties. Carrie Tingley Hospital later moved to Albuquerque, New Mexico, under the administration of the University of New Mexico.

144 *Somewhat confusingly* "Famed Naturalist Awaits Birth of Child," *New Mexican*, June 11, 1938, and "Mrs. Seton Denies Story of Child," *New Mexican*, June 13, 1938.

144 *Within a few months* Seton and Julia hired a babysitter to travel with them, Pablita Velarde of Santa Clara Pueblo, who not long afterward emerged as a leading Native American painter.

145 *Seton's other publishers* Seton had failed in his attempt to sell a book about dogs in the military. When that larger project failed, he published *Santana*, a short story, as a small book. The printing of five hundred copies sold so poorly that I was still able to purchase a copy from the Seton Museum in 1972 for just a few dollars.

145 *During the summer* Hall to Julia Seton, an undated series, summer 1946. Condolence letter, Hall to Julia Seton, October 27, 1946, Seton Papers, Library and Archives Canada.

146 *In September* Wallace, "Wild Animals He Has Known."

146 *he recited the prayer* Stephen M. Jessup, "A Tribute to Ernest Thompson Seton, Santa Fe, New Mexico—October 25, 1946." Seton Papers, Library and Archives Canada. Original music in Seton, *The Book of Woodcraft*, 145.

147 *a remarkable statement* Seton also discussed the ethics of Native Americans in his essay "Spartans of the West," published as part of both editions of the *Book of Woodcraft and Indian Lore*, 1913, 1923.

148 *He and Seton shared outrage* "The Indian Question," undated document, Seton Papers, Library and Archives Canada.

148 *it was in "The Buffalo Wind" essay* Seton wrote this essay sometime in the 1930s; he had at least two hundred copies of it printed and bound with a buffalo-hide binding to commemorate two events that took place on August 14, 1938. One was his seventy-eighth birthday. The other was a ceremony for baby Beulah that took place at the Woodcraft summer camp. My consideration of the mystical aspects of Seton in *The Buffalo Wind* and *Trail of an Artist-Naturalist* was greatly aided by critical insights from two students of Seton's work, Robert G. Hare and David Braddell, in a series of ongoing discussions and correspondence. They pointed out specific passages scattered through Seton's late work that the naturalist seems to have left, purposely or not, as clues to his most intimate character. Hare wrote of the Red Man's River as "a metaphor for the ego voluntarily dissolving into the Cosmic Ocean." He has speculated that the deeply emotional reactions Seton experienced from hearing certain winds or visiting certain places may be described in Hindu terms as involuntary Kundalini seizures, and that the journey Seton describes in the essay is not a physical one at all, but a spiritual one. We cannot know the discussions held between Seton and Manly

Hall, but perhaps the young philosopher introduced the old naturalist to theosophy as a way to explain the Buffalo Wind.

149 *"the Indians of Shasta"* The Shasta Tribe faced disaster when the region was overrun by gold-seekers in 1850.

149 *"The book dropped"* Hare to author, February 25, 2008: "This is the clearest statement that the Wind is his code for mystical epiphany. I know from my own experience that when the spirit takes you, you can fall to your knees or find your muscles suddenly 'frozen'—I can see ETS sitting there with his book, some line he was reading sent him into a cognitive dissonance and while the ego-mind is stalled out his soul fills the void. He goes into a sitting trance and the book falls."

Appendix 1

153 *In 1823, after the general amnesty* Seton discusses his ancestry in a section entitled "The Name of Seton" at the end of his autobiography, *Trail of an Artist-Naturalist*, 391–93.

153 *Lord Seton and Earl of Winton titles* Burke, *Genealogical History*.

153 *Joseph's letter to George Seton* Joseph Logan Thompson to his son, George Seton, May 14, 1901. Courtesy of Clemency Chase Coggins.

154 *ETS could have claimed* ETS's eighteenth- and nineteenth-century ancestors are charted in "Our Family Genealogy," compiled by "W.S.T.," September 12, 1912, in Toronto. This may have been William Snowdon Thompson, Joseph's second oldest son. Courtesy of Clemency Chase Coggins.

154 *The Setons are essentially* Robert Seton, *An Old Family*, 1.

155 *Sir William Wallace* Among sources consulted for general background on Wallace, Bruce, and Scottish and English history, three were especially helpful: D. J. Gray, *William Wallace: The King's Enemy* (New York: Barnes & Noble, 1991); Colm McNamee, *The Wars of the Bruces: Scotland, England, and Ireland, 1306–1328* (East Lothian, Scotland: Tuckwell, 1997); and Winston Churchill, *A History of the English Speaking Peoples*, Vol. 1 (New York: Bantam, 1963).

156 *Three hundred years later* Robert Seton, *An Old Family*, 36.

157 *"Lord Winton's character"* Ibid., 118.

157 *There have been claimants* Ibid., 121.

Appendix 2

158 *"The West of which I speak"* Thoreau, *Collected Essays and Poems*, 239.

158 *"When we try to pick out"* Muir, *My First Summer in the Sierra*, 245.

Index